Vanessa Jones · William R. Jones · Maxine Karam · Joan Kaufman · David N. Kay · Patrick Keetley · J. Andrew Keller
Collen Kelly · Elizabeth Kelly · Kaci Kepferle · Michelle Klevan · Stephan Knight · Meaghan Kroener · Yeehing Lam
Palmer Lane · Paul Langland · Manuel Lauzurique-Abiega · Doug B. Lee · John Lenkin · Cornelius Ives Lister, Jr.
Gregory Loman · Jeffrey Loman · Johnny A. Maas · Michelle Lopez-Orsini · Glenn MacCullough · Jeremy Mack · Ben Maddox
W. Clark Manning · Yolanda Marina · Gerald Marshall · Leslie E. Mason · Nasir Masood · Lisa Matey · Robert C. McClure
Melissa Mileff · Travis Miller · Dan P. Moseley · Jonathon H. Moss · Fiona E. Muelken · Gabrielle M. Muise · Abdul Muzikir
John N. Nammack · Matt Neumann · Sean Nohelty · John J. Nolis · Steven K. Nose · Hayes Nuss · Brian O'Looney
Matthew M. Ossolinski · Roland O. Pepin · Theresa Petramale · Todd S. Phillips · Stacey R. Phillips · Pier D. Pierandrei
Julia Pilipovich · Chris Pizzi · Matthew Poe · William Poulos · Juan Francisco Prieto-Arbelaez · James Ramsey · Joseph Rapazzo
Peter Reiger · Jon A. Reinhard · Donna Rendelman · Diana S. Reuter · Johnathan Rich · Ariane Risto · Jon Eric Ritland
Noemi B. Riviera · Kimberly Rollings · Stephen Saff · Pedro Sales · Christopher Salvadore · Muhammadali Sami · Bruce W. Sanford
David M. Schwarz · Jeffery Scott · Elizabeth Shepard · Evan G. Siegel · Kimberly P. Simons · Bjorn Slate · Ken D. Smith
Timothy K. So · Sean Stadler · Thomas J. Stodghill · Stephen Strasser · Mike Sutton · Michael Swartz · Shalini Taneja · Heather Tarner
Barrie Teach · Ken Terzian · Jefferson B. Thomas · Erik Thompson · Ronald Tomasso · Jane Treacy · Mark Van Brocklin
James M. Vanderputte · Jeff Van Houten · Phillip Wagner · Douglas Ward · Magda Westerhout · William H. White, III · Craig P. Williams
Jeffrey E. Wilson · Mark E. Wouters · Yuehui Xu · Joy Yoder · Richard Zambito · Mojgan Zare · Jon Zubiller · Lauren E. Zuzack

DAVID M. SCHWARZ/ARCHITECTURAL SERVICES

1976–2001

DAVID M. SCHWARZ/ARCHITECTURAL SERVICES

PREFACE BY VINCENT SCULLY

INTRODUCTION BY ROBERT A.M. STERN

PROJECT TEXT BY BRADFORD McKEE

Art Direction: James Pittman

Copyright © 2002 by:
David M. Schwarz/Architectural Services. Inc.
1707 L Street, NW, Suite 400
Washington, D.C. 20036
Tel: (202) 862-0777
www.dmsas.com

Grayson Publishing
James G. Trulove, Publisher
1250 28th Street NW
Washington, D.C. 20007
Tel: 202-337-1380
Fax: 202-337-1381
jtrulove@aol.com

Hardcover ISBN: 0-9679143-6-1
Softcover ISBN: 0-9679143-7-X

Printed in China

First printing: 2002
1 2 3 4 5 6 7 8 9 / 03 04 05

We at Architectural Services would like to thank all our clients over the last 25 years who have allowed us to express our thoughts about architecture and the built environment in their projects.

We would also like to thank writer Brad McKee and publisher James Trulove for letting us make an acknowledgment in this book.

CONTENTS

Post Postmodern

The career that David Schwarz has carved out since 1976 seems a remarkably traditional one, as if begun some 75 years earlier. The work itself would fit in well with the buildings and the urbanism of that era and is, in general, distinguished from them mainly by its Modern interiors and by a certain repetitive hardness, rather metallic in character, that reflects the intervention of the Modern era as a whole. It has none of the cartoonish exaggerations of Postmodernism, whatever that ambiguous term may have meant, or the preoccupation, really High Modernist in origin, with hectic originality. Instead, it seems to take itself unselfconsciously for granted and has its own hard-edged style or touch, whether having to do with Gothic Revival, Mediterranean Revival, Modern Classic, or Art Deco forms: a panoply that any solidly eclectic architect of the period 1900 to 1930 might well have displayed with pride.

Probably the most interesting thing about all this is that none of it seems in any way remarkable to Schwarz. He is not in revolt against Modernism, is in no way polemical. The style wars of the later twentieth century are long over for him. He seems simply to be doing his work as it comes along, and that work has been shaped by some particular conditions that are themselves more traditional than canonically Modern in character.

First, there is place, in Schwarz's case, two places: Washington, D.C. and Fort Worth. The early buildings seem to grow directly out of Washington, out of Schwarz's respect for Washington's urban structure and architectural traditions. So from the beginning, for which, one might add, he was prepared by his architectural education at Yale, Schwarz was ready to design buildings that would fit in with the buildings around them to enhance Washington's architectural fabric rather than to outrage it. They consistently avoided High Modernism's adversarial pose. Schwarz seems to have been working unashamedly within the parameters of a society he respects. So his buildings are without irony. They might have been there always, and that stance led Schwarz naturally on to a fundamental concern for Historic Preservation and, eventually, to the New Urbanism, which is represented by several schemes in this volume.

Then came Fort Worth and after it, apparently, a good deal more of Texas. But here another traditional element appears: The Client, and a client out of the historical past, one not merely an employer but an informed protector and friend, like the patrons of the Renaissance. This is Edward P. Bass, whose involvement with architecture, like that of the rest of his family, is much deeper and more passionate than that of most contemporary clients, though, here, in a very different context, Robert Davis of Seaside also comes to mind. But loyalty to an architect seems to occur naturally to the Bass family. Edward Bass's brother Sid R. Bass remained devoted to Paul Rudolph long after most of Rudolph's American clients had fallen away, and he commissioned some striking buildings, including a distinguished house, from Rudolph in his later years. Another Bass brother, Robert M. Bass, served as chairman of the National Trust for Historic Preservation. Edward Bass, like the rest of his family, has poured his concern for preservation, rehabilitation, and community building into his own city of Fort Worth, with David Schwarz as his architect. Work has ranged from new neighborhoods and apartment complexes to the Nancy Lee and Perry R. Bass Performance Hall, where rangy limestone angels, 48 feet high and lifting long, golden trumpets, rise spectacularly to flank the entrance.

Schwarz's work is all of its place, and again, curiously, of its time—a time, which Modernists like to think of as having passed, but which, so far, has refused to die. Though the Ballpark in Arlington is part of a new urban grouping assembled by Schwarz, it reminds us of the old urban ballparks of around 1900, and along with the new ballpark in Baltimore, its precedent has played an important role in the building of city-center stadiums once again. Baseball: Hardly a modern game at all, neither murderously megalopolitan like professional football, nor a sinister perversion of higher education like the college brand, but the incurably rustic product of an older America of densely settled, highly competitive cities, each the half-built polis of a people not long from the farm—a crucible of energy by no means exhausted, into which David Schwarz has been perceptive enough to tap.

Robert A.M. Stern

Tradition and context have liberated David Schwarz to be really effective as an architect. In Schwarz's work, the governing mantra is that of suitability, familiarity, rather than self-importance. He imaginatively adapts time-honored models to contemporary conditions. His use of tradition does not derive from an antiquarian's love of the past, or from that of a sentimentalist, but from a sense that the lessons of the past can help him address the underlying psychology that lies behind so very many of today's building programs. Holding onto the inherent formal properties, the grammar and syntax, and even the composition, of buildings from the past, he modifies them, remaking them for a new set of circumstances, which he has very carefully studied and to which he responds in a highly nuanced way.

David Schwarz is perhaps the most prolific among a small but significant number of architects now entering their maturity, who, finding twentieth-century Modernist architecture and urbanism an insufficient basis for their work, have turned to traditional architecture. I say turned, not returned, because these architects were trained in Modernism and they have had to retrain themselves in the formal languages that preceded it—that is, the high language of classicism and the many regional vernaculars. Schwarz came to an appreciation of traditional architecture's contemporary efficacy as the result of his time at the Yale School of Architecture, in the early 1970s, when, in the aftermath of the social and artistic upheavals of the late 1960s, he was exposed to the probing but gentle discourse of the idiosyncratic architect Charles Moore, the knowing enthusiasms of the scholar-architect Allan Greenberg and the ornamentalist Kent Bloomer, and the contextual urbanism of David Lewis. Most important was the broad humanity of Vincent Scully, whose impact was deep and enduring, opening up the young architect to the widest view of architecture, its possibilities, and, above all, its responsibilities to the public and to popular taste.

Schwarz, who was part of a class that included Andres Duany, Elizabeth Plater-Zyberk, and Patrick Pinnell, each of whom has importantly criticized the prevailing Modernism and the frequently tiresome heroics of its advocates—though in fairness, the anti-heroics can become pretty tiresome as well. Impelled by the example of their teachers, these young architects put aside many of Modernism's overworked tropes—particularly its technological dandyism and its cult of the visually obscure, in favor of a celebration of traditional and vernacular architecture, in which the quirky works of everyday buildings were as valued—if in different ways—as the masterworks of the high styles. This repository of architecture has been misconstrued as an attempt to return to the past—that is, to roll the clock back. But these Yale-trained architects, not least among them Schwarz, are very modern, with full appreciation of the realities of the times. They take the past and the vernacular as a jumping-off place for invention; they regard the past as a repository of ideas capable of further development. Of this group Schwarz sees the past in somewhat strategic terms, adapting precedents to more effectively solve modern problems—that is, to engage the public and the context as he builds.

After Yale, Schwarz spent some time in New York working in the office of Paul Rudolph before moving to Washington, D.C., in 1976, where he developed a precocious practice specializing in new buildings that were sympathetic to the District's residential vernacular, the mostly Gothic-derived row houses of the late nineteenth century, the preservation of which was then a much-contested battle as the city's appetite for apartment houses and office buildings grew ever more insatiable. Schwarz met that market with new buildings that had a character distinctly reflective of and suited to the context. Schwarz's bold modern version of the District's Gothic was diagrammatic and a bit raw, as so much of the Posmodernist work of the period was, but it was head and shoulders above most of the other preservation-friendly stuff being built at the time. It was individual and contextual. More recently, as his work has taken him to Texas and Florida, Schwarz has become a master of thematically evocative public architecture, hitting his stride as an architect with crowd-pleasing buildings that reinforce and enhance programs and places. For example, his modest addition to Fort Worth's public library had a transformative effect on the public's perception of that institution: what had been little more than a supermarket for books, built beneath a street-level parking lot, was transformed by Schwarz into a dignified public institution that says "public library," not only with words but with the symbolic associationalism of its skillfully composed, affordably realized classical façade.

His Bass Performance Hall has proven itself successful as that most elusive of all building types, a multipurpose auditorium—a catch-all approach that rarely adequately satisfies the requirements of the various artistic disciplines it seeks to accommodate. Bass Hall succeeds not only as a performance venue for opera and dance companies, symphony orchestras, and popular entertainers of all stripes, but also as a place of celebratory gathering that can turn an evening at the theater into an occasion. Set amid Fort Worth's Sundance neighborhood, with many red-brick vernacular buildings restored by Schwarz, as well as new ones designed by him, including tall apartment blocks and small-scale shops, not to mention the blockbuster glass-skinned office towers designed by Paul Rudolph in the 1970s, Bass Hall fills its city block in the way that the old Metropolitan Opera House did in New York. At first glimpse Bass Hall is a bit overwhelming—a bit, dare I say, "over the top"?—with its heralding angels thrusting themselves out over the street. But this is a theater, not a city hall, so why not? Closer inspection and, especially, direct experience of the carefully orchestrated procession of interior foyers leading to the jewel-box

hall itself show them to be superbly executed and perfectly calculated to extend the drama of the performance. The ivory-colored hall, with its specially designed appointments, is elegant but not so much so that it can't work for popular as well as elite entertainments.

Schwarz's deep feeling for what the culture expects in a building type comes through nowhere better than in the Ballpark in Arlington, which has the look, the feel, and the sound of the kind of home to baseball, such as Fenway Park in Boston, that most fans admire. Unlike Fenway Park, or the long-ago destroyed but still lamented Ebbets Field in Brooklyn, both of which were models for Schwarz, and both of which were tightly embedded in their urban sites, the Ballpark in Arlington is unfortunately marooned in open country so that it does not have the capacity to interact with the wider community. For this reason, it suffers a bit by comparison with Camden Yards in Baltimore. But close comparison between these two excellent examples of cultural contextualism reveals that Schwarz's design grapples far more completely with the tectonic implications of its genre—much more than a nostalgic wrapper on a modern stadium, it is a true reinvention of the type.

No matter the medium or the sources of inspiration, self-expression is part of all creative activity, so that a designer, working with traditional forms, is not bereft of a distinct voice. Schwarz's voice is bright and clear. His mode of expression is blunt, with not too many grace notes, though he appreciates the value of ornament—instilled in him by Kent Bloomer—revealing a fine sense of what flat patterns can do to help scale down the whole. This sense for surface embellishment can be seen to very good effect in the diaper patterning of the brick walls of the recently dedicated Environmental Sciences Center Building at Yale, the first Gothic-style building constructed at the university in two generations. The Environmental Science Center complements Day & Klauder's Gothic-style Peabody Museum of 1926 to which it is attached and partly interconnected. The use of the Gothic is not only important as a simple act of contextual courtesy, but has important implications for Yale as it embarks on a significant expansion of its facilities for the sciences, many departments of which are housed in Gothic-style buildings of the 1910s and 1920s designed by Delano and Aldrich and others and in stylistically sympathetic but functionally constricting Modernist buildings designed by Philip Johnson in the 1960s. Because Yale's fundamentally Gothic character has served departments in both the humanities and the sciences for a century, frequent alienation between these two disciplines is much less apparent than at other institutions. Schwarz, who benefited from the sympathetic support of his patron, Edward Bass, challenged the prevailing wisdom that equates stylistic Modernism with scientific research and designed a Gothic-style building that, instead, appropriately expresses Yale.

The Environmental Science Center shelters some of Schwarz's best interior spaces. The octagonal tower that is the building's principal exterior feature is quite worthy of its many precedents in the collegiate Gothic tradition, but it turns out not to accommodate a stair, as one might think. But there is a grandly spatial octagonal stair, nonetheless, just to the side, an odd condition but one that works. More inventive—innovative, even—is the 150-foot-long slit down the building's length that not only opens up the interior to natural light but also creates an opportunity for the scientists in their labs, and the anthropologists attached to the Peabody Museum in theirs, to each work in perfect acoustic and environmental isolation, yet to meet on the stairs and in shared halls, and, most importantly, to glimpse each other at work across the light-filled void. Schwarz's building literally supports a community of scholars.

Each of us, as we leaf through monographic studies such as this, must keep in mind that every building, no matter the style, familiar or not, is an experiment the success of which cannot be measured in glorious photos or after a few short weeks' use, or by an occasional visit, but by the test of time and evolving experience. Buildings are not just for the here and now, not just for the titillation of an opening night with its accompanying media blitz, or for a flashy spread in a glossy publication, but for the long haul. I am happy for this book, which gives readers a chance to consider the work of David Schwarz carefully for what it is and what it is not. Here are buildings that contribute to cities, rather than compete with them. Here, indeed, are plans for cities, or at least parts of them, that in their simple clarity make for useful, civil environments. David Schwarz is that rarest of architects—a popular architect. He builds for the public, which returns to him and to his clients the high accolade of sympathetic appreciation.

Imagine that!

ROBERT A.M. STERN

1718 CONNECTICUT AVENUE

Washington, D.C.

1979

People who walk regularly in this busy shopping block of Dupont Circle have come to regard the office and retail building at 1718 Connecticut Avenue NW as a landmark, despite its being a relatively new building. Designed in 1979 and completed in 1982, it offers an object lesson in the contextually acute architecture for which the firm has since become widely known. It was a breakthrough design—not merely for the architect but also for the Dupont Circle neighborhood and, indeed, for the city of Washington— because as an example of neighborhood preservation, it sets as much precedent as it

follows with an inventive response to an eclectic urban environment.

At the time of its conception, in 1979, the city had recently passed a tough historic-preservation law, one of the first of its kind in the nation, and guardians of the newly designated Dupont Circle Historic District had yet to test fully that statute's powers to protect the community's character. But the design of 1718 Connecticut did not resist the new preservation rules; it capitalized on them. The design took inventory of the neighborhood and offered up a critical synthesis of its historic rhythms and textures, turning constraints into opportunities and winning approval from preservation officials upon its first review.

The developer needed a big building on a fairly small site. Thus, in maximizing the allow-

able floor area, the firm chose a clever disguise, expressing the building's mass as a suite of three modestly scaled bays facing the street—each articulated at the width of a typical townhouse—crowned by gables (cf. 1722 and 1724, the pair of buildings just to the north) and a mansard roof at the fifth floor. The volume containing the sixth and seventh floors is set back on a terrace behind the lower of two mansards and delineated at its attic by a broken cornice and a shallow arch. Lining the terrace is a two-story row of windows within the frames of brick arches upon stone-capped piers. The upper mansard connects two corbelled brick towers as bookends. To the south, a clock tower, which holds elevators, rises above the streetscape, its pyramidal roof visible from several blocks away. A smaller

First floor plan

1. Office lobby
2. Retail space

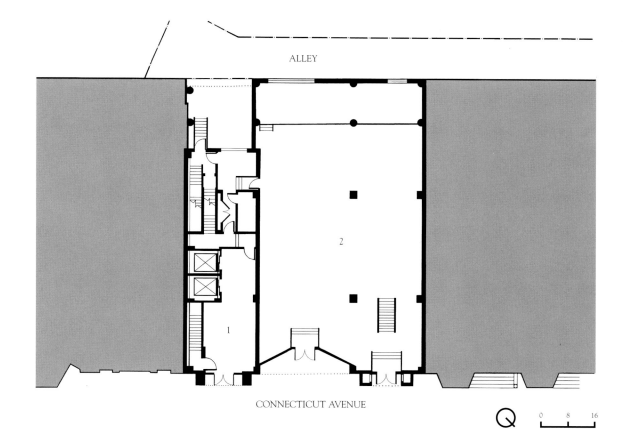

ALLEY

CONNECTICUT AVENUE

0   8   16

Opposite: Connecticut Avenue Façade. East elevation of 1718 Connecticut breaks into articulated bays to diminish apparent scale at streetside. Material patterns of neighboring buildings echo rhythmically in brick and limestone bands, varied arched portals, roof gables, and flush cornice and roof lines.

Right and far right: Models. Hand-crafted paper models show northwest and southwest views of rear elevation.

Below: Rear Façade. West elevation of 1718 Connecticut addresses context of stuccoed alley façades in International Syle idiom, reinforcing the eclecticism of Dupont Circle Historic District. Ribbon windows and bowed bay recall Le Corbusier.

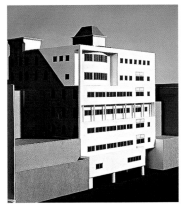 

Right: Terrace Façade. Fifth-floor setback creates sixth-floor terrace. Molded brick walls and ironspot brick arches face terrace upon brick piers, whose contrasting limestone caps connect them visually.

Below: Brick Corbelling Detail. Brick corbelling and sawtooth borders of 1718 Connecticut towers extrapolate local examples of masonry detailing.

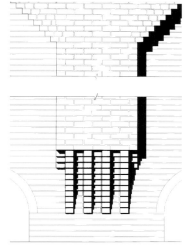

tower to the north, containing mechanical equipment, contrapuntally balances the composition. The façade's contrasting materials merge the substance and details of adjacent buildings by abstracting or simplifying their forms. Brick details pick up the patterns of townhouses directly north. The buildings adjacent to the south inspired the façade's bright limestone bands and casement windows. The window heights and cornice lines of 1718 match those of adjacent structures and seem to complete the block with musical regularity, an effect that the deeply punched windows reinforce.

This building has not one face, but two. If the main façade reinterprets neighborhood designs, its alley or western façade of white stucco suggests another building

entirely. This laconic object follows a purely 20th-century tradition, with ribbon windows that approach those of Functionalism and a subtly hemicyclical bay at the upper floors that recalls the *brassieres* of Le Corbusier. The character of 1718 Connecticut manages to be both humane and sculptural at once. From the summit of Connecticut Avenue a few blocks north, the profile of the upper floors quickens the streetscape by amplifying the apparent depth of the block. The façade's rich patterning marks the way memorably along a major pedestrian thoroughfare. And the unmistakable silhouettes of the towers stand prominently on the local skyline. These manipulations of mass render a building of several complex parts, one that simultaneously exploits and submits to its environment.

Section

1. Office space
2. Retail
3. Parking

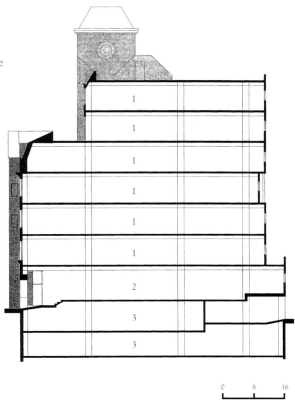

Sixth floor plan

1. Office space
2. Terrace

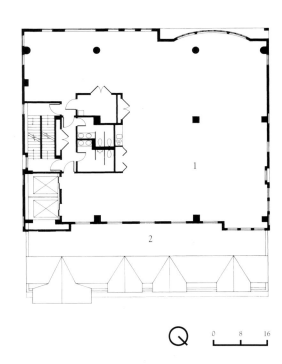

Left: Entrance to Lobby. Main entrance on 26th Street NW stands between two Tuscan columns, the lines of which continue up through piers of balcony screen wall. Detail grows more intimate in scale as one draws nearer to the entrance. Limestone entablature and surrounds frame the brass door beneath horizontal limestone bands and cast-bronze sculpture of a winged lion.

Above: West Façade. West elevation of the Griffin steps down to assimilate itself between two zoning districts of distinct scales, from gabled volumes standing at full 90-foot height along K Street NW to 70-foot bay with bowed crown and, finally, 50-foot bay with gable, matching the scale of the Foggy Bottom residential district. Heavy moldings divide base, middle, and top. Alternating fenestration patterns, including punched screen-walls, reduce apparent mass facing park.

THE GRIFFIN

Washington, D.C.
1982

The Griffin's job is a diplomatic one. It brokers an elegant accord of massing and scale between two distinct zoning districts, the blockbuster scale of downtown Washington's K Street office corridor and the residential dimensions of Foggy Bottom, flattering both neighborhoods without favoring one over the other. It follows what became a quintessentially successful strategy of the firm: Let the city shape the building as the building shapes the city.

The careful form of the Griffin acts as the western gateway to hard-edged K Street, where it looks out over the natural swale of Rock Creek Parkway and, beyond it, Georgetown and the Potomac River. It is a large building that makes itself instantly obliging with a clear organization of its base, middle, and top (the middle pronounced by a somewhat darker brick than the matching base and top), and a skyline that Washingtonians find familiar—five bays of the L-shaped structure face north onto K Street, approaching the full 90-foot height limit.

Two gabled towers bracket three half-hexagonal bays with mansard roofs, the same forms on which the sun and shadows play in many D.C. neighborhoods.

The southern leg of the building takes gentle steps down in scale as it makes the transition toward the townhouses of Foggy Bottom. The 90-foot-tall mass becomes a 70-foot mass, then a 50-foot mass. This is where the building creates multiple readings, where materials and cornice lines vary—is it one, two, or three structures? Across the façade, intense vertical lines of light and shadow cross the horizontal break metal cornices delineating its three parts, and the building appears to be a relaxed, organic assemblage of several properties. Deeply punched balcony openings strike the bass notes of this composition, in counterpoint to the solid brick fields, which are all reflected color. Those balconies, in turn, draw copious doses of daylight into the condominiums (the units of the northern bays rotate eastward 45 degrees for more comprehensive views).

The grid of open porches reveals a common design approach of the firm, wherein structural elements carry their maximum meaning. The porches not only provide interior light and look interesting from afar—they also mark the building's entrance, meeting the ground upon a formal, discreetly recessed doorway between spare Tuscan columns. The detail diminishes in scale as you approach the entrance, keeping the building ever in range of human perception.

Site plan

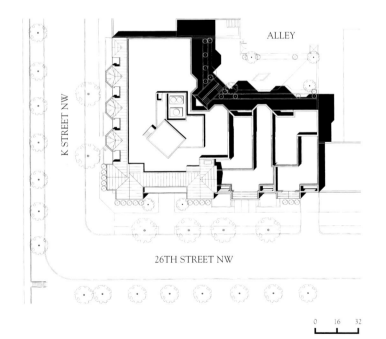

0   16   32

Typical floor plan

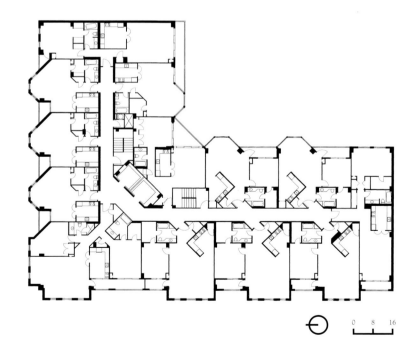

0   8   16

RETREAT RESIDENCE FOR A SUBURBAN FAMILY

Washington, D.C.

1983

In this apartment overlooking Rock Creek Park atop the Griffin, dramatic chevron vaults thrust upward from corner gables to the roof, expressing the outer form in compound angles above the living room. The firm designed this apartment as a pied-à-terre for a collector of modern furniture, who wanted to give each piece on display the space it needed and still have room to throw a good party. Thus, with clean edges and minimal detailing, the structure does most of the talking. In the kitchen, as in the living room, the roof plane folds inward for complex reflection and deflection of daylight. A long, skylit barrel vault floats ethereally over the balcony terrace facing west between two bays that complete the formal public axis of the apartment. The living quarters comprise three bedrooms, among them a master suite for sitting and sleeping, a playroom, a study, and a generous terrace facing south. The contours of the space frame the collection in broad, spare strokes that keep the refinement of the craft furniture in the foreground.

Floor plan

1. Foyer
2. Living room
3. Dining room
4. Kitchen/family room
5. Master bedroom
6. Dressing room
7. Master bathroom
8. Dressing room
9. Bath
10. Study
11. Powder room
12. Playroom
13. Bedroom
14. Bedroom
15. Maid's room
16. Terrace

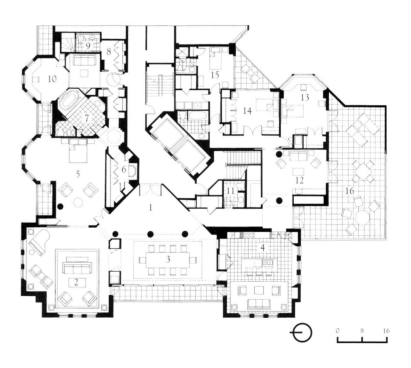

Opposite: Living Room at Dusk. Interior of apartment at top level of the Griffin expresses structure where perpendicular gables intersect. Angular planes resolve in chevron folds that reflect ambient light from ocular windows onto collection of modern craft furniture.

Opposite: Dining Room. Barrel vault opens balcony terrace, on axis between living room and kitchen, to light and air. Open side walls create cross-axis with entrance foyer, framing extended westward views from deep interior space toward Rock Creek Park and Georgetown.

Right: Sink and Shower in Master Bedroom Suite. Diffuse backlighting escapes a translucent sandblasted strip in bathroom wall mirror, providing soft, indirect illumination. Countertops are granite and curve outward gently.

Far right: Tub in Master Bath. Frosted glass transmits daylight into raised tub of master bath from an adjacent study. Surrounding pattern of black granite wall tiles provides backdrop to black granite tub deck and countertops.

Bottom: Kitchen. Compound geometries collide in kitchen roof plane, bending light onto bare wood floor with eccentric inset of black vinyl beneath minimalist white island. Doors open to playroom and rear terrace.

RESIDENCE FOR AN ART COLLECTOR

Washington, D.C.

1983

In an apartment on the eighth floor of the Griffin, this client, a bachelor, wished to display a collection of large-scale paintings and sculpture. Diagonal walls within a restricted floor plate create the longest possible surfaces for their presentation. Within the major grid governing the apartment's plan, three repeating modules of perpendicular walls rotate 45 degrees. These configurations also allow the eye to travel well beyond the immediate room and transfer daylight softly to the deepest interior. The superstructure of the space expresses itself frankly in four interior columns that define the living room; these columns hold integrated lighting that projects onto the walls, from which it reflects indirectly back into the living space. One column, in the video room, forms half an armature for the housing of a retractable projection screen, which is compellingly rendered as a truncated cornice floating just far enough below the ceiling plane to reveal its independence from the structure. The cornice's opposite end rests upon a slender Corinthian column, an atavistic presence that, in this modern space, provokes reflection on the ancient lineage of modern design.

Floor plan

1. Foyer
2. Living room
3. Fireplace sitting area
4. Sitting area
5. Video room
6. Study
7. Dining room
8. Kitchen
9. Master bedroom
10. Dressing room
11. Master bathroom
12. Guest room
13. Terrace

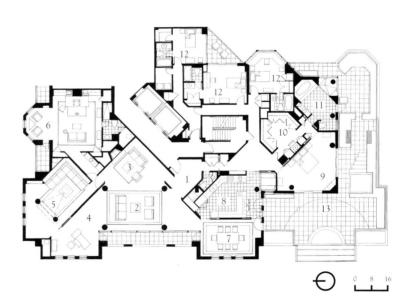

Opposite, top: Fireplace Sitting Area. Heavy circular columns intercept planes of angled walls, which are positioned to maximize hanging area for paintings. Columns contain integral lighting strips that wash light evenly toward walls and art works.

Opposite, bottom: Living Room. Four columns frame seating area of living room. Angled wall extends sight lines toward daylight penetrating adjacent dining room.

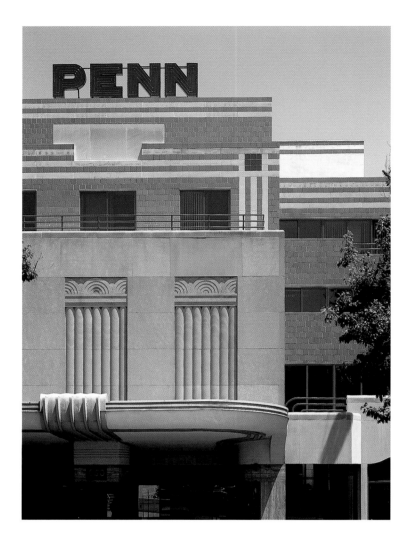

PENN THEATER PROJECT

Washington, D.C.
1984

The Penn Theater Project represents an act of neighborhood preservation, wherein the objective is not to rescue a particular building as such but to preserve the contribution of the building's spirit to the diversity of its environment. This set of buildings in Washington's Capitol Hill Historic District, totaling 101,000 square feet, has proved, as new construction, every bit equal in vigor to the stately (and varied) architecture of the neighborhood. The firm designed the office, retail, and 35-unit residential development around the limestone marquee of an Art Deco movie house on Pennsylvania Avenue SE a

few blocks from the U.S. Capitol—a historic building in a historic district, certainly, but not a designated landmark. The theater itself didn't merit saving, but the marquee and adjoining stone storefronts did, and the architect used that armature, along with surrounding clues to the neighborhood's past, as a guidepost in designing the new complex.

The broad, four-story Penn office building animates its block of Pennsylvania Avenue with a lively reinterpretation of 1930s Deco clad in sky-blue-glazed brick. The massing of the 45,000-square-foot office building surrounds the marquee frontispiece symmetrically with two lateral wings that extend forward as terminal towers. From the marquee came inspiration for façade details such as the sculptural cast-polymer spandrel panels

between windows, the patterns of colored tiles and stone stripes upon the brick, and the Streamline red tracery highlights upon the dark glass.

The residential north half of the Penn Theater Project pays homage to the vibrant, venerable Eastern Market, across C Street SE, with compound hipped and gabled roofs atop a brick façade economically detailed with horizontal stone bands radiating out at arch height above the first-floor entrance. Like many of the firm's finest works, the apartment building helps the streetscape digest the mass of a large building into several smaller-scaled components, and provides ample punctuation for the eye to follow in cast-stone lintels and window surrounds.

The courtyard between the buildings is a subtle exercise in urban planning, naturally rec-

onciling the awkward angle left between the radial avenue and the gridiron side street. If the two buildings contemplate the architecture of their respective streets, the triangular courtyard between them departs into a Mediterranean abstraction like that of Alvaro Siza. Upon a quiet plaza of fountains and planters bounded by angular white walls, a shining white concrete screen projects outward from the apartment building at full height before stepping down along the courtyard. This screen mediates between and provides privacy to the façades of the office and apartment buildings and makes a monumental gesture that neither building claims exclusively. It completes an intelligent—and intelligible—ensemble that takes stock of its surroundings and renders unexpected but sympathetic forms.

Site plan

1. Office lobby
2. Office space
3. Courtyard
4. Apartment lobby

Opposite, top left: Detail of Pennsylvania Avenue Façade. Façade detail shows limestone ribbons scoring the edges of blue-glazed brick body in Art Deco patterns harmonic with preserved limestone marquee of original theater building.

Opposite, top right: Office Building Façade Detail. Cast gypsum spandrel panels between windows elaborate relief carved into limestone marquee.

Opposite, bottom: Pennsylvania Avenue Façade. South elevation of Penn Theater office building, with lateral wings pulling forward to bracket the marquee at center. Note the way upper-story details reinforce the building's intimate scale on historic block.

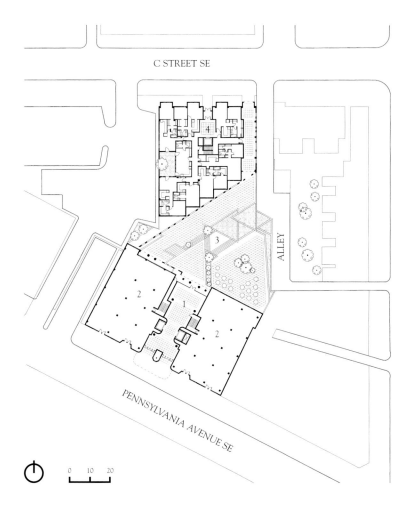

C STREET SE

PENNSYLVANIA AVENUE SE

0   10   20

Opposite, top: Model of Court-yard. Model shows courtyard between office building and apartment building. Garage entrance lies below a series of terraced planters.

Opposite, bottom: Courtyard Detail. Courtyard's multiple levels serve the street and lower office levels as well as apartment building. Stairs connect planters and fountains situated at various elevations.

Top: Model. This model view shows apartment building articulated with projecting bays to provide street rhythm and scale compatible with neighboring row houses.

Bottom: Apartment Building Street Façade. North elevation of apartment building shows street façade, with details that refer to historic motifs in nontraditional arrangements.

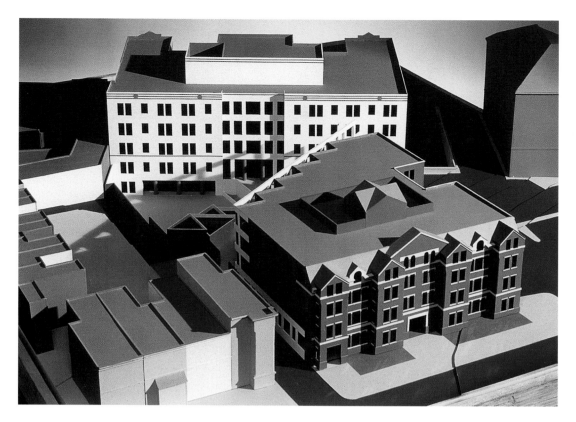

1818 N STREET

Washington, D.C.
1984

It is easy not to notice the surgical intervention of 1818 N Street NW sitting behind a row of late-19th-century vintage townhouses near Dupont Circle. But once you do spot the 130,000-square-foot office building, you may hardly detect the graceful graft of the large new volume to the

smaller, more domestic façades (without their original party walls, for structural reasons), because the new building seems wholly deferential to the history of the block, though it has a decidedly modern beauty and integrity of its own.

If preservationists worried that the scheme for the building would harm the block's ornate house fronts, surely they were instead heartened by the ways it bolsters the houses' presence by counterpoint. The overarching strength of 1818 N Street is its sympathetic massing, which has the new building buttress the townhouses at their four-story height on the north side of the site and then gently climb up to meet the large commercial scale of the ungainly office buildings behind it to the south and east.

At street level, the building's plan basically forms a solid block inserted behind the old façades. The "front" of 1818 comprises those painstakingly restored façades, and one enters the building through a central portal whose pilaster-and-entablature frame distinguishes itself by its larger scale and relative simplicity, compared with the ornate detailing of the townhouse bays and their heavy iron stairs.

Above the fourth-story townhouse gables and mansards, 1818 turns sculptural. Light and shadow play upon its articulated bays, and the mass steps back in a series of three terraced levels delineated by shallow pediments and parapets. The collective impression of 1818's upper silhouettes is like that of an Italian hill town: an organic, dynamic grouping of peaked

roof forms whose symmetrical ordering appears delightfully random from the oblique angles available to pedestrians on the street.

The red-clay-colored brick of 1818 serves to highlight the paler hues of the houses, and the new structure's simplified details—bands of blush-colored precast concrete—identify it firmly but don't compete with the older buildings' rich, eclectic ornament.

The building's polemic is a calming one—it proves what is possible in a city that has sacrificed its share of historic architecture over the past few decades. It adds visual value to the block as a mask, a foil, and as an object, and responds to the spontaneous rhythms and geometries of earlier generations without trying to upset their place in history.

Opposite, top: View of Northwest Corner. Sculpted massing upon a square footprint renders 1818 as a collection of structures gradually reconciling the lower, historic scale of row houses to the higher-density office blocks to the south and east.

Opposite, bottom left: New Terraces Above Townhouses. Stepped terraces and gabled pediments of 1818 N create backdrop to gables of historic row houses. Simply detailed, deep-rust-colored brick offsets brighter, more highly ornamented façades in foreground.

Opposite, bottom right: West Façade. At west elevation, the building's full height expresses itself frankly; lighter cast stone bands upon articulated bays reduce the mass to recognizable proportions.

North elevation

Floor plan

1. Office lobby
2. Office space

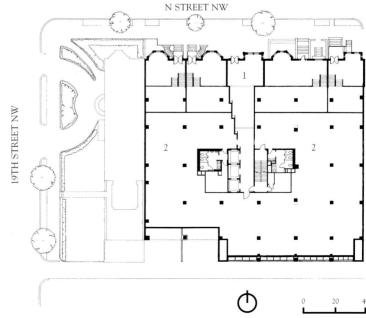

COOK CHILDREN'S MEDICAL CENTER

Fort Worth, Texas

1985–Ongoing

Of all the complicated, large-scale projects the firm has undertaken, perhaps none has had as much emotional content as Cook Children's Medical Center, near downtown Fort Worth. The story of this design unfolds in several dimensions. On the urban scale, the building represents the merging of two old-line institutions, Cook Children's Hospital and Fort Worth Children's Hospital, and it had to carve out a strong identity on two city blocks at the faceless edge of the city's medical district. It had to create context in a place where context was largely intangible, consisting mainly of institutional memory. At the scale of the block, it was imperative that

the campus plan generate the activity of a community, like a self-sufficient village. And to that village environment come multiple constituencies—families, doctors, nurses, therapists, teachers, and clergy, not to mention administrators and benefactors—bringing multiple priorities, some overlapping and others conflicting, but all of them focused on the care of children who are ill, many critically or terminally so.

The event of the merger compelled the client to express in its new building a combined legacy of community service, to project both permanence and a progressive spirit. The hospital didn't need a new architectural image as such—indeed, the staff of the 60-year-old Cook Children's Hospital were only reluctantly leaving their beloved if obsolete Italian Renaissance limestone home. Thus the architectural language

of this 321,000-square-foot complex is formal—reminiscent of early-20th-century stripped Classicism as exemplified by Paul Philippe Cret or Bertram Goodhue—but it incorporates fantasy and whimsy in a way that is childlike without being childish.

The six-story main hospital anchors the complex at the eastern half of the site, facing west over a large, gently sloping parterre garden thickly shaded by live oaks and studded with crape myrtles and Winnie-the-Pooh topiary. Adjoining it on the south is a recently opened outpatient facility. A new clinical wing with 71 beds (for a total of 264) on the north side will complete the site's northeastern corner next to the low-rise administration building. Across West Terrell Avenue to the south stands a 1,008-car parking facility with whimsical

battlements defining the parapets—it can also be reached via a Renaissance footbridge.

The hospital's symmetrical massing and façade details all direct visitors to the front door, which stands at the base of a central tower beneath a low-slung porte-cochere whose proportions suggest Prairie-school architecture. It is a large building, seven stories at the central tower's full height, but its tripartite delineation upon stone cornices and balustrades above the second and sixth floors reduces the scale to human proportions. Vertically, too, the mass steps back twice from the central towers before extending north and south to six-story hyphen volumes that link to lateral towers. Two-story pavilions, further broken into stoical bays, reach forward on either side of this main building. All of these principal volumes culminate in bright

Opposite: Main Entrance. Central massing of west elevation conjures memory of Beaux-Arts former hospital. Hierarchy of details—window rhythms, tile squares, balustrades—focuses the eye on the main entrance beneath central canopy bracketed by lanterns atop two stripped, slender pylons.

Top: Site Perspective. Main hospital on east half of site anchors formal arrangement of gardens and ancillary buildings. New south wing of expansion appears directly south (*right*) of hospital, with castle-like parking garage just across street. New clinical wing will replace original Fort Worth Children's Hospital building directly north (*left*) of hospital. Administration building occupies corner in   foreground.

Bottom: Entrance Façade. Formal parterres and topiary line drive to main hospital entrance. Quiet meditative garden lies to south of drive, with active play garden to north. Low-rise pavilion at right brings scale of complex to human proportions.

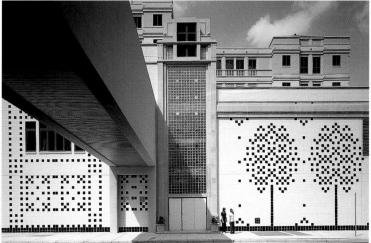

Opposite, top: View from Parking Garage. Series of lantern-topped pylons hold floating canopy to cover walkway toward hospital from south.

Opposite, bottom left: Bay Windows at Cafeteria. Cafeteria faces south to draw light into gridded-glass bays of dining area. Pilasters on base reinforce human scale.

Opposite, center right: East (Rear) Façade. Glazed-brick patterns incorporate tree designs to add interest to windowless emergency wing, where pedestrian bridge meets hospital.

Opposite, bottom right: Bridge to Existing Building. Masonrylike pedestrian bridge iterates castle-and-fort fantasy motif of hospital complex and connects new building to 1961 Fort Worth Children's Hospital building.

Below: Southwest Corner with Bridge. South extension of hospital's cafeteria and laboratories meets street edge at manageable pedestrian scale with subtly articulated bays. Bridge spans West Terrell Avenue, connecting south garage and Pediatric Professional Building.

blue pyramidal roofs that reinforce the building's hierarchy, as does the classically phrased fenestration—windows in rows of five on the central tower resound in rows of four, and then pairs, on the wings as the eye travels outward. Red tile squares and blue window mullions offset the wall surfaces, offering another index to the building's scale from the sidewalk.

Children's hospitals are singular environments in that they need to heal patients, but also, in varying degrees, must soothe, stimulate, and even entertain them. To that end, the architect arrayed nursing and treatment units around a fantastical full-height atrium colorfully rendered as a town square. It is like no space the kids have ever seen, with a pastel assemblage of bays, towers, and stacked loggias reflected in trompe l'oeil by mirrored curtain wall grids.

Near the atrium's roof, the space expands by 12 feet wider than the floor area to steal maximum amounts of daylight through a transparent glass roof framed by heavy white ridge-and-valley beams. Marble and granite slab paving patterns the sunny commons below, which is usually busy with people eating, talking, or celebrating special occasions.

From the atrium, the doors to lateral corridors have abstractions of pediments applied above them, as if to point the way ahead, which the firm made sure would never be a dead end. The lower two levels contain surgery, intensive care, and outpatient care along north-south corridors connected by auxiliary halls. The circulation makes sense to even the most distracted visitor, owing to several integrated methods of marking space in which graphics become part of the decoration for the architecture. Navigation occurs within

a child's sight lines—pastel-paneled nurses' stations, detailed with colorful blocks as finials, stand at the center of each ward at a height of 30 inches so patients can easily approach them, and cartoon pictograms identify various departments. Corridors become more intimate with simply stenciled frieze details and enfilades of arched doorways. Natural light penetrates crucial parts of the building, such as the outpatient waiting area and the emergency room, where a wall-sized, interactive aquatic diorama dominates the space. Patient rooms emphasize normalcy—with medical hardware discreetly hidden, they almost seem like home (and each furnishes a bed for parents). The design of this hospital refines a more enlightened approach to healing children—it goes extra lengths to make itself accessible to them, to be a place that they, above all, can trust.

Typical floor plan

1. Atrium
2. Playroom
3. Elevator lobby
4. Nurses' station
5. Waiting room
6. Conference room

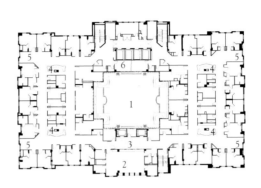

First floor plan

1. Porte cochere
2. Entrance vestibule
3. Atrium
4. Gift shop
5. Volunteer office
6. Physical therapy department
7. Orthopedic clinic
8. Bridge to original hospital
9. Nuclear medicine department
10. Radiology department
11. Trauma center
12. Ambulance entrance
13. Emergency department
14. Emergency waiting area
15. Cafeteria
16. Admitting
17. Pulmonary clinic

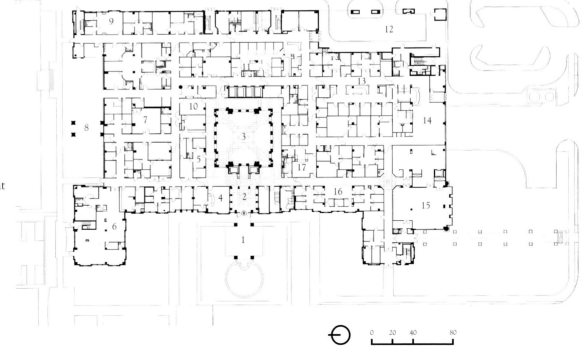

0   20   40   80

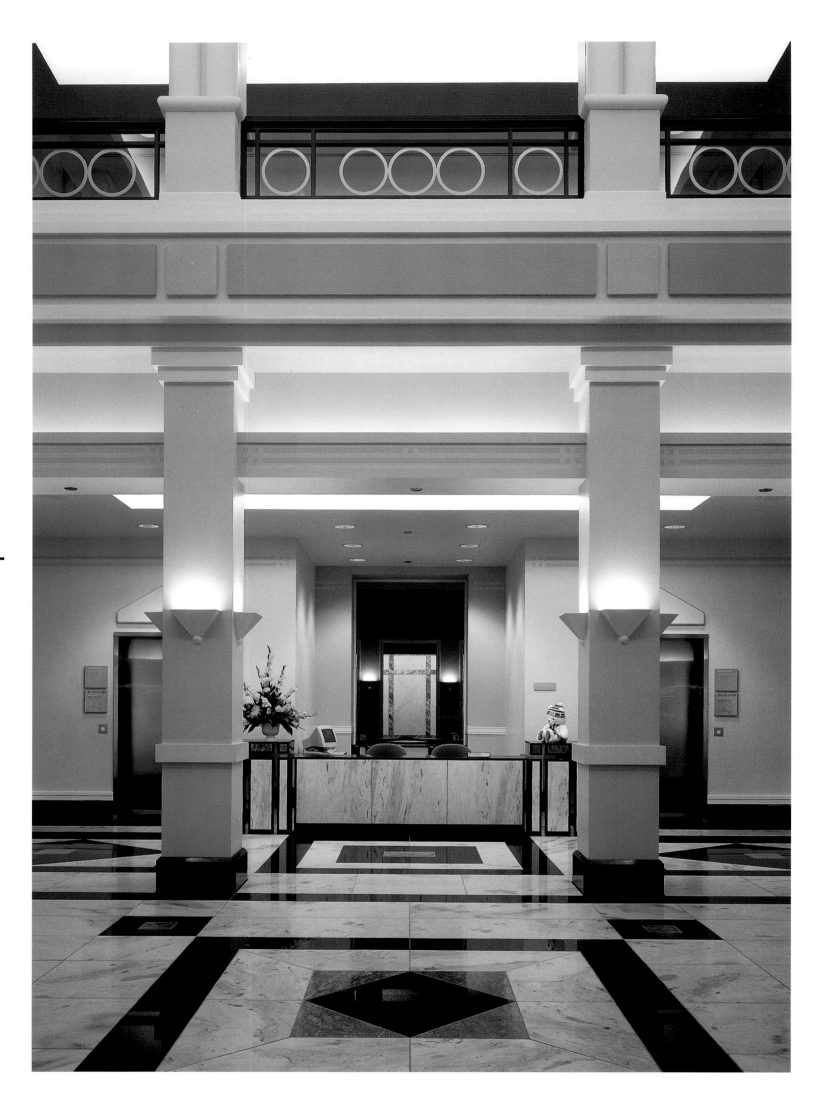

Opposite: Entrance Vestibule. Patterns of marble-and-granite-paved entrance lobby direct visitors toward information desk at center, flanked by elevator banks. Interior detailing of column bases and capitals, along with sconce uplights, mitigates grand scale of lobby, making it accessible to children yet dignified for adults.

Top: Typical Patient Ward Corridor. Nurses' stations stand at central cross-axes of patient wards. Low counter height makes approach easy for children. "Building-block" finials brighten the clinical environment.

Below and bottom left: Pictograms. Illustrated pictograms of "Little Russell" character identify departments. Pictograms hang at child height for easy navigation by patients.

Bottom right: Stencilwork and Signage at Patient Room. Stencil-card signs (holding nursing information and child's name) and sconce lighting mark doors to patient rooms. Clean, bright surfaces and cornice moldings domesticate the space.

RADIOLOGY

PATIENT REGISTRATION

Opposite and top: Parking Garage. Simple, economical parapet battlements create memorable image for parking garage.

Bottom: Mechanical Plant. Central mechanical plant's horizontal bands and clean surfaces furnish Bauhaus counterpoint to classically articulated hospital volumes.

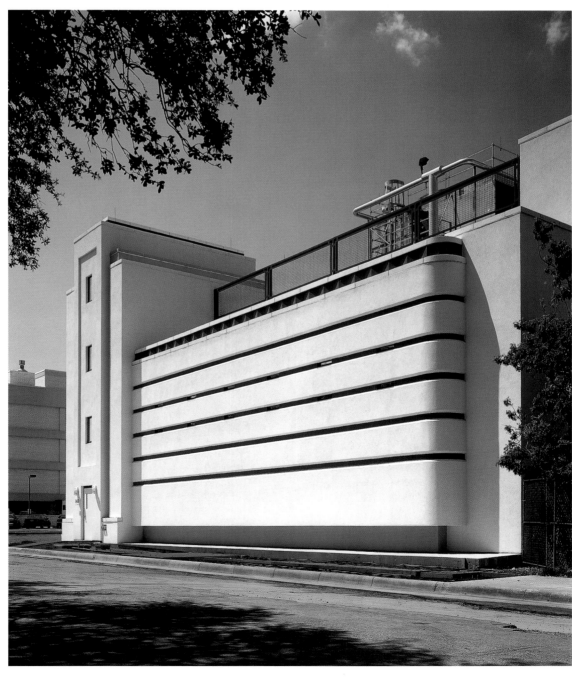

THE SARATOGA

Washington, D.C.
1986

Several generations of grand apartment houses have risen along Connecticut Avenue NW from Dupont Circle to Chevy Chase since the 1920s, varying in style from various Renaissance revivals to neo-Georgian to Art Deco. The 292,000-square-foot Saratoga represents a latter-day triumph of this venerated Washington lineage—and it was the first nonsubsidized rental property developed in the District in 20 years.

The Saratoga bows to its avenue forebears even as it turns the building type into an entirely contemporary proposition, an essay of light and shadow drawn in long, frank lines on a tree-shaded corner. The front portions of the building's two towers step back along the angle of Connecticut Avenue. The building's complex massing, taken after that of the 1940s Chesapeake apartment house next door so as to continue the rhythm of the street wall, offers both bold, vertical grandness as well as more intimate grace notes where the building meets the ground, particularly about the cloistered entrance.

The building's base, middle, and top are clearly discernable. At the street level, horizontal stone bands help to bind the tower to the land and define a human scale, which is reflected in the stone sills and lintels of the windows above. Plaid patterns of cast stone play upon brick fields across the upper and lower façade, animating its gabled bays, which are coupled with chimneys that domesticate the tower's upper profile.

The Saratoga's north-facing units rotate 45 degrees eastward to frame the view toward Rock Creek Park and onto a classical garden enclosed by the ell of the north tower. The deeply punched balconies steal light from the façade to create color contrasts within a regular grid. Along the south façade, these apertures, stacked in pairs, open between undulating three-sided bays to form a complex exterior fabric that suggests the dynamic of individual households within.

Site plan

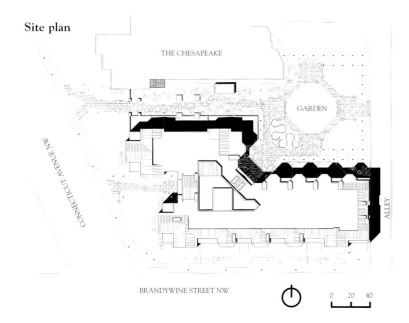

THE CHESAPEAKE

GARDEN

CONNECTICUT AVENUE NW

ALLEY

BRANDYWINE STREET NW

0   20   40

THE SARATOGA

0   20   40

Opposite: Corner of Connecticut Avenue and Brandywine Street NW. South elevation shows intensive patterning of base and upper stories, which temper the building's massive scale—as do articulated, gabled bays and punched screen-wall marking formal main entrance.

Above: Site plan shows the Saratoga's footprint stepping back southward away from street to continue rhythmic set by Chesapeake apartment building directly north. Classical garden lies in east crux of site.

Above right: South elevation shows rhythmic gables and chimneys atop attenuated bays.

Left: Connecticut Avenue Façade. Bold limestone and brick patterns delineate formal base, middle, and top of Saratoga building (shown at northwest corner).

Opposite, top: Main Entrance. A stone portal within another portal marks formal main entrance.

Opposite, bottom left: South Façade. Undulating façade creates strong streetside rhythm, with articulated bays alternating between punched windows of screen walls.

Opposite, bottom right: Northeast Façade. Rear of building encloses formal garden above entrance to parking garage. Bays of north-facing units rotate 45 degrees for broader eastward views.

Floor plan

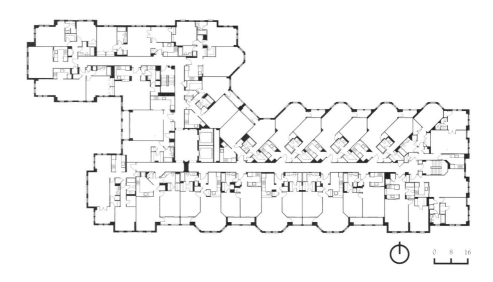

MANHATTAN APARTMENT

New York City, New York
1987

In 1987, the firm designed the interior of this 1,800-square-foot apartment on the 33rd floor of Park Tower (designed by architect James Stewart Polshek) to display the client's large collection of craft furniture art. The commission called for restraint. The space announces its identity only in the elegant, functional detailing of floors, walls, and fixtures, to keep the focus of attention on the furniture's presentation.

Floors throughout the apartment's living spaces have walnut and wenge borders around expanses of rock maple. The circular entrance hall's floors of walnut, maple, and brass form a sunburst pattern offset by accents of black granite and lapis. This hall, with a plaster dome ceiling completing its circular form, provides a turning point from the elevators to the public areas of the living room, dining room, and kitchen, to a corner den, or to a central corridor leading to the private quarters of the apartment. Between the entrance hall and the living room, a diagonal wall slices through the orthogonal grid to amplify the size of the space, provide an engaging plane for the art works, and segregate the den and dining rooms on either side without enclosing them. The wall's diagonal also extends the reach of natural light entering through north and east windows.

The deep, full-length frames designed around the nearly square windows emphasize their verticality. To create more pleasing proportions, each major window has a smaller window module beneath it, next to a pane of frosted art glass lit from within. Custom casework fills the lower portion of window alcoves with granite sills atop it. Above these windows runs a floating crown molding that serves as a light cove. Where structural columns interrupt the cornice, mitered sconces repeat the cornice forms upon the column.

The simple detailing of the kitchen, which adjoins the dining room and the central corridor on either side, favors the clean, cubic profiles of lacquered cabinetry and $1\frac{1}{2}$-inch-thick black granite countertops. Flush cabinet doors have touch latches in lieu of surface hardware, and the cabinets themselves seem to float above mirrored backsplashes that help open the space visually. Floors of checkerboard granite and marble ground the black-and-gray interplay of cabinets and counters.

The bedroom's appointments defer to the windows' view toward Central Park. The contemporary master bathroom shares the kitchen's contrasts of black counters (in marble) and white cabinets leading back to a custom slab-granite Roman soaking tub. Mirrors have frosted glass reveals to temper the lights behind them. An adjacent dressing room seemingly expands in volume in the reflections of strategically placed mirrors.

The furniture collection requires state-of-the-art climate control, for which the firm specified computer-controlled, low-voltage switching systems, motorized blackout shades, museum-quality humidity control, and the cove lighting. An atmosphere of simplicity and quietude unites the rooms of this apartment, and the furniture collection benefits greatly from the design's minimal inflections.

Floor plan

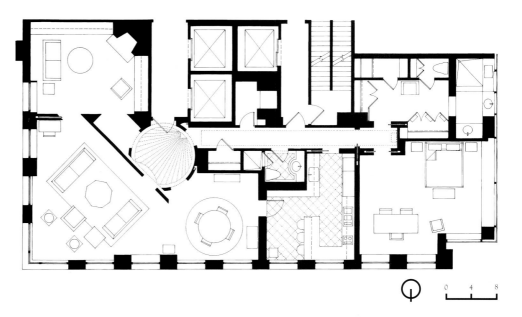

Opposite: Living Room. Minimalist detailing of apartment interior highlights collection of furniture art. Windows are set deep into wall plane within full-length frames that enhance their apparent height.

Left: Entrance Vestibule. Circular entrance hall's floor comprises custom-inlaid walnut, maple, and brass in sunburst pattern, with walnut and wenge borders.

Below: Corridor. Central corridor leads to private quarters, beneath square recessed light.

Opposite: Dining Room. Dining room, with view into kitchen at rear, has cove uplights that furnish indirect illumination above floating crown molding.

Top left: Master Bathroom Vanity Detail. Master bathroom vanity of lacquered casework sits beneath mirror detailed with frosted-glass strip lighting.

Top right: Powder Room Detail. Powder room holds bowed sink with black marble countertop.

Left: Master Bathroom Detail. Master bathroom contains custom slab-granite soaking tub.

Opposite: Kitchen. Clean lines of unadorned casework and dark-and-light surface contrasts define kitchen.

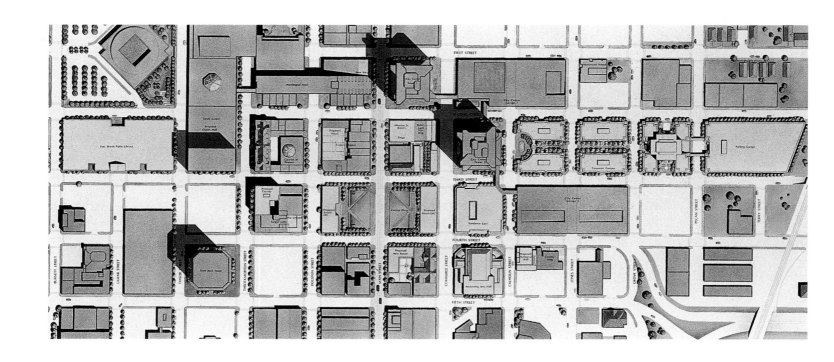

FORT WORTH MASTER PLAN

Fort Worth, Texas
1988

In 1988, the firm began working with a group of concerned local property owners to revitalize the heart of central Fort Worth. The city's historic downtown, like many across the nation, had succumbed to suburban economics after World War II. Destructive planning practices common in the postwar period made Fort Worth a less safe, less walkable, and less convenient place to live and work and play, whereas the suburban development became increasingly accommodating to a rapidly expanding population. Many of the city's problems were psychological—anxieties about crime and traffic were matched by a lack of commercial and cultural activity—but most of those were rooted in symptoms of physical atrophy. Traditional storefront buildings had fallen to make way for parking garages that darkened the streetscape, or for surface lots that frayed active, orderly block edges. In addition, there were numerous obstacles to walking around the district, discouraging pedestrian flow even in a relatively compact downtown with small, 200-foot-square blocks. The firm began a series of studies within a 30-block area centered on historic Sundance Square (though the plan contemplated 150 blocks as significant context). The aim was to regenerate downtown as an around-the-clock residential, commercial, entertainment, and cultural core by knitting back together disparate but vital areas of the district. As shown by several projects on the following pages, the strategy so far has been an enormous success.

Initial phases of the firm's studies documented viable uses, property ownership, historic buildings, building densities, open space, transit, and traffic patterns with three-dimensional computer models. Following those inquiries, the firm analyzed pedestrian behaviors and attitudes to determine real or perceived barriers to walking within the city.

Based on these findings, the plan's next phase began to specify potential types, locations, and densities of new development. Downtown's growth had skewed southward, and the firm's studies determined that it was critical to draw new development back toward the center and northern parts of downtown near the historic courthouse and as far north as the Trinity River.

Of particular importance, the firm found, was the role of Third Street, the only east-west downtown street without dead ends or overhead spans of multiblock buildings that could tie together the east and west sides of downtown. Among the first recommendations was to turn Third Street from a one-way to a two-way street and develop its edges with a mix of uses.

Among the highest programmatic priorities for the downtown district was to repopulate it with households. This realization inspired new residential development at the west end of Third Street, as well as the Sundance West apartment building and the Sanger Lofts projects. At the outset, the plan indicated that a critical mass of approximately 500 residential units would help fuel corollary business and cultural uses in the district. The success of the first two projects stimulated much more development. To date, more than 1,200 units have been completed, exceeding those early projections.

Third Street also benefited from the expansion of the Fort Worth Central Library Building, which helps connect downtown's western edge to the commercial core, where two new multi-screen theaters and a variety of retail stores and restaurants have helped restore downtown's street-level business base. A new cultural economy has grown, too, around the arrival of the Nancy Lee and Perry R. Bass Performance Hall and the adjacent Maddox-Muse Center.

Today, the success of the firm's vision for downtown Fort Worth is evident in several dimensions. Several once-empty or tattered blocks now hold lively rows of storefronts. People walk the streets of the city at all hours and feel safe, and there are plenty of basic services, specialty stores, and a wealth of dining and entertainment possibilities on a scale that did not seem possible in this downtown for decades. The plan's comprehensive scope engendered a symbiotic collection of social and economic improvements on which the city will continue to build for years to come.

Opposite, top: Downtown Core Plan. This plan of historic downtown core indicates physical disposition of downtown's Sundance Square area, suggesting juxtaposition of existing and potential uses.

Opposite, bottom: Three-Dimensional Computer Model. Computer-generated axonometric model of downtown shows variation of density and open space in central plan area around Sundance Square.

Right: Planning Diagrams. These study diagrams helped the firm to diagnose specific issues inhibiting pedestrian activity in downtown Fort Worth. Clockwise, from top left, are maps showing streets visually cut off by building and block closings, unbuilt block areas, pedestrian unfriendly block edges, and historic buildings and properties.

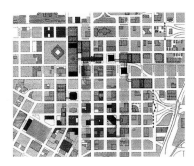

DAVID M. SCHWARZ/ARCHITECTURAL SERVICES

SUNDANCE WEST APARTMENT BUILDING

Fort Worth, Texas
1988

A renaissance began in downtown Fort Worth's historic Sundance Square district with the completion of the Sundance West Apartment Building and adjoining cinema complex (pages 60–63) in 1992. For the firm, this project begat a rich career of city-building in conjunction with the Bass family of Fort Worth. It was the first piece built in the master plan (cf. p.55).

There are 69 apartment units on the seven upper levels of the 12-story Sundance West tower, stacked atop one floor of retail space and four floors of cinemas. To mitigate the shift in scale between downtown's smaller historic storefront structures to the south and east and the much larger Tandy building and Worthington Hotel on the west and north, the architect developed the parti as a stepped cluster of independent structures whose formal frequencies vary—it looks, in effect, pleasantly unplanned.

The building manages this transition with detailing that grows more complicated from bottom to top. Simple, bold cast-stone bands hug the base, whereas the gabled and terraced summit appears busier (and thus nearer than it might otherwise) with its polychrome brick patterns and cast-stone relief panels of distinctly Texan origin.

At street level, the detail directs you to the main entrance on Throckmorton Street, located at the center of the building's bays under a shallow metal arch perched atop two metal cornices. The detailing of the lobby suggests Texan gentility, with patterned marble tile, fair-colored raised-wood wainscoting, and heavy white columns, cornices, and moldings. Cattle heads etched into the brass elevator doors and mounted as column capitals nod to Fort Worth's cowtown history.

The apartment interiors are, for the most part, clean and simple, with rotated walls in some units stirring a largely orthogonal plan. The angled walls bend daylight toward the interior from casement windows and punched balcony openings. Several units open onto crenellated terraces that underscore the gables and two-tiered chimneys, animating the roofline with human purpose.

West-east section

1. Cinema lobby
2. Cinema 6
3. Retail level
4. Apartment levels
5. Parking levels

Opposite: Main Apartment Building. West elevation of Sundance West apartment building (in sunlight) faces Throckmorton Street with street wall that recedes quietly back from center of structure. Fenestration revives rhythms of historic structures around Sundance Square.

This page: West-east section (*near right*) describes integration of lower-floor retail program beneath residential tower, extending full block length. Site plan (*far right*), shows position between low-rise historic structures to east (right in plan) and modern high-rises to west (*upper left in plan*). Massing, seen in elevations (*bottom*), makes transition by shaping Sundance West complex as a cluster of independent structures buttressing each other.

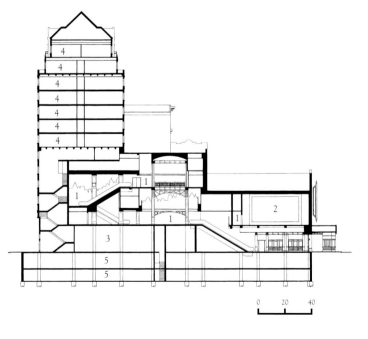

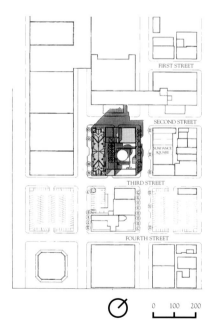

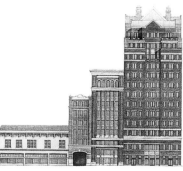

Floor plan

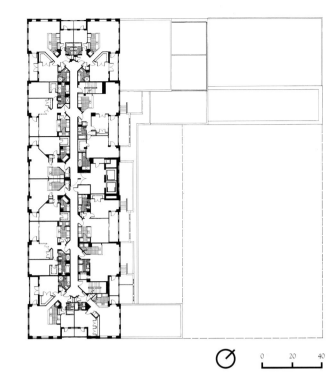

Opposite: West Façade Detail. Interlocking volumes activate roof profile. Skyline details of polychrome brick give Sundance West local character.

Top left: Entrance Detail. Perpendicular lines of façade details intersect at main entrance to apartment building, which stands beneath articulated canopy.

Top right: Apartment Building Lobby. Patterned marble floors, columns, and crown moldings distinguish formal lobby.

Right: Elevator Door Detail. Cattle head embossed on elevator door continues native cowtown imagery found throughout Sundance West.

SUNDANCE AMC ELEVEN CINEMAS

Fort Worth, Texas
1988

Inside and out, this 11-screen cinema complex harks back to a time when popular culture—film and comic books particularly—celebrated the heroic beauty of the American city as a demi-monde of glamorous towers and millions of twinkling lights, a place where progress was ever-imminent. The Sundance AMC Eleven Cinemas was born of a kindred faith in Fort Worth—and the moral imperative of good urbanism to bring people back downtown.

Such a development, though, seemed risky here in 1988; this was the first multiplex to open in a Texas downtown in many years. But the investment paid off handsomely: Sundance West became the region's busiest theater, and one of AMC's busiest in the nation.

The lobby was conceived as a set for an imaginary 1930s Busby Berkeley musical. Moviegoing becomes a passionate event again as you walk beneath the marquee and vertical neon sign on the Art Deco façade and into the escalator lobby, where a backlit skyline illustrated in etched-glass panels emerges against a nightscape of electric-blue walls that gradually brighten to twilight hues and then dim again, by virtue of a theatrical lighting system. Another set of escalators leads to an upper lobby between "riveted" metal columns joined by an arched truss right out of Hugh Ferris's reveries. This nostalgic urban futurism recurs in the four-story lobby. A wall-sized mirror doubles the apparent size of the interior. Corridors leading to theaters are also lined by mirrors and etched-glass tower figures. You also find this theme in the theaters themselves, where a series of panels bearing skyscraper silhouettes mark the space's increasing depth between sconces, whose light diffuses onto the walls.

West-east lobby section

1. Street lobby
2. Main lobby
3. Upper lobby
4. Lower projection level

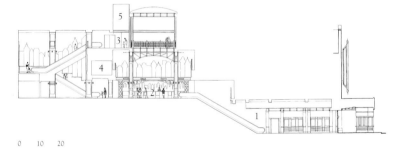

0   10   20

Opposite: Cinema Entrance Façade and Marquee. Art Deco façade serves as frontispiece to interior cinema complex, its scale sympathetic with historic block. Projecting marquee shelters entrance.

Right: Cinema Street Lobby. Entrance lobby introduces riveted metal motif that appears throughout cinema complex.

Far right: Main Lobby and Escalators to Street Lobby. Etched-glass panels of skyscraper forms hover above and to the sides of escalator lobby. Arched truss connects riveted metal columns.

Floor plan

1. Cinema 1
2. Cinema 2
3. Cinema 3
4. Cinema 4
5. Cinema 5
6. Cinema 6
7. Four-story lobby
8. Concessions

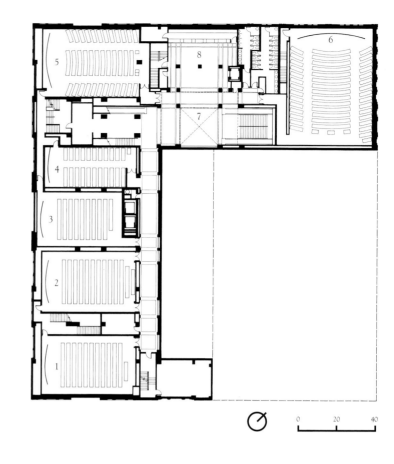

Opposite, bottom left: Main Lobby. Four-story-high main lobby space contains large metal-clad columns in each corner. Mirrored wall doubles both the volume visually and the etched-glass cityscape imagery.

Opposite, bottom right: Upper-Level Concession Stand. Concession stand on upper-level theater terrace bears Art Deco details.

Right and above: Upper-Level Stair. Newel posts of stair railings elaborate modern-Gotham sensibility of Art Deco–inspired interior.

1133 CONNECTICUT AVENUE

Washington, D.C.
1989

Opposite: Detail at Street Level Looking South. Building base reads as two-story building with attic, clad in Indiana limestone with stylized classical details. Neo-Classical fenestration marks office entry at left, with bracket-supported pediment and steel-and-glass canopy.

Below: Southwest Corner. View of southwest corner shows façade wrought as a classical base, shaft and top composition. Shaft portion subdivides into masonry piers with punched windows, which delineate fields of highly articulated curtain wall with copper-clad major mullions to emphasize the building's verticality.

When the firm began designing 1133 Connecticut Avenue at the obtuse corner of DeSales Street in 1987, it had to pay particular attention to the landmark Mayflower Hotel. The Mayflower, completed in 1924, is the grande dame of Farragut Square, and the firm wanted to salute its heavy masonry, old gold, and dowager glamour while paying sufficient attention to the newer glass-and-granite office buildings across Connecticut Avenue. But the handicaps were these: The new building was to be a curtain-wall structure whose massing entirely filled the zoning envelope, which precluded complex sculptural manipulations to match the bowed towers of the Mayflower and its punched windows. Moreover, the anchor tenant at street level would be a department store,

which meant that the exterior needed clear visual encoding to disclose the building's dualistic purpose of retail and office space. The object, as the firm saw it, was to reflect the Mayflower's scale, depth, and detail in a building that would yet assert its modernity through contemporary means of construction.

The rounded-corner massing of 1133 restates the Mayflower's shallow bow, and the tripartite logic of the exterior speaks largely to the Mayflower as well. The three lower floors of the limestone-clad base stand almost as a low-rise building unto itself, perfectly approachable to pedestrians with store-front bays set into a girdle of two-story-high pilasters and metal spandrels, all engaged beneath a third-floor attic of deeply punched windows topped by a balustrade.

The base's neoclassical vocabulary overlaps with the contemporary idiom of the building's middle: Four limestone window surrounds reach up to the fourth and fifth stories, contrasting sharply against fields of dark glass curtain wall—delineated by orderly mullion grids—to create the illusion of relief. The glass fields alternate with piers of brick and pre-cast concrete up to the 10th-floor cornice. Above the cornice, the building's upper two stories iterate the historicist fabric of the base and harmonize with the crown of the hotel.

The presence of the department store in the lower floors posed two peculiar problems, the first being that it wedged the office lobby and elevators into the northern quarter of the site, and the second being

that the building would need two entrances, one for offices and one for retail. Therefore, the firm makes the hierarchy between these approaches clear: The retail lobby, though at the prominent corner of the building, received minimal elaboration, whereas one enters the office lobby beneath an ornate canopy of metal and scalloped glass. The canopy hangs from heavy limestone brackets beneath a simple pediment, with a central arched window and two small sidelights at the second-floor level. The exterior grammar of 1133 Connecticut, like that of all the firm's most urbanistic projects, orients pedestrians and tells them exactly where they are and what to do.

Opposite: Office Building Lobby. Main office lobby consists of a series of coffered spaces leading to elevator core, which recedes deeply owing to configuration of ground-floor retail space. Concierge desk at apselike terminus marks turning point to elevator lobby (not seen at right rear).

Top: Elevator Lobby. Elliptical geometry resolves angle of elevator core (see plan, right), which arose in response to Connecticut Avenue's angle relative to the cardinal street grid.

Right: First-floor plan shows retail space occupying most of the footprint, which places office lobby at northern perimeter of building. Lobby paving patterns continue into sidewalk.

First Floor Plan

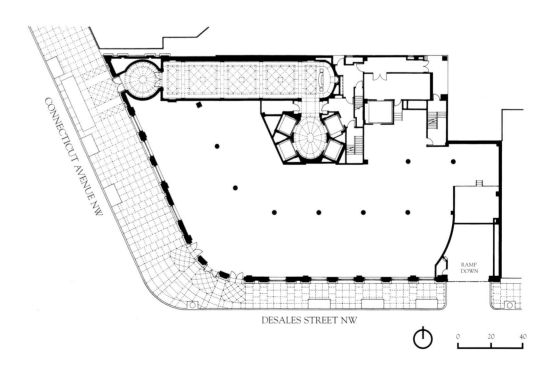

CONNECTICUT AVENUE NW

DESALES STREET NW

RAMP DOWN

0   20   40

INVESTMENT FIRM OFFICE SPACE

Washington, D.C.

1989

Restrained luxury permeates this suite of offices for an investment firm in Washington, designed to recall the city's old-line legal and banking institutions but with simplified details wrought in a brighter palette of materials. The highly stylized Neo-Classical design begins in the elliptical elevator lobby, where mostly flat wood wall panels incorporate three types of maple inlaid with fine stripes of mahogany and ebony accents to resemble traditional stile-and-rail assembly. This lobby leads through French doors to a reception area centered toward the rear by a reception desk whose wood panels, pilasters, and cornice lines summarize the texture of the interior as a whole. A shallowly recessed space steps back behind the desk between a pair of engaged columns. The juxtaposition of various shapes in the floor plan resolves the junction of two grids that govern the building's structure, a scheme arising directly from the obtuse angle at which the orthagonal DeSales Street meets the radial Connecticut Avenue. The interior arrangement creates an active flow from one grid to another—the rectangular reception area opens into a hexagonal vestibule (one instance where coordination of lighting and air ducts allows the ceiling plane— here a domed rotunda—to exceed typical heights), which leads to a fan-shaped common area, an oval principal office built into the bow of the building, a row of offices fronted in a maple-and-glass curtain wall, and a kite-shaped office at the building's northern corner. The wainscoting, interior columns, coffered ceilings, and floating crown moldings holding uplights do not return to past architectural forms so much as they bring the past up to date.

Floor plan

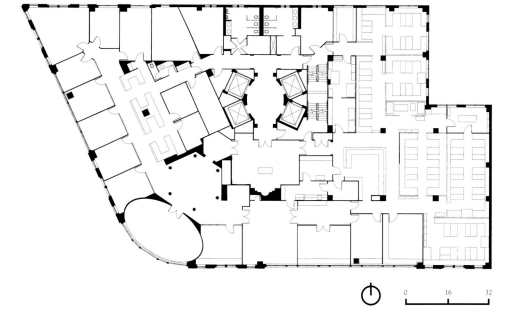

0   16   32

Opposite: Reception Area. Reception area holds custom-inlaid maple reception desk, reflecting woodwork found throughout the suite.

Above: Central Space. Hexagonal central space marks juncture of two circulation spines— entrance from reception area and entrance from principal office. Freestanding maple columns in Tuscan style stand at corners of hexagon beneath maple entablature.

Opposite: Circulation Spine. Typical offices divide from spine by way of interior maple-and-glass curtain-wall system. Natural light from offices penetrates inner corridor and administrative spaces at left.

Right: Principal Office. Elliptical form of principal office translates exterior curve of building's southwest corner, and, ultimately, geometry of street angles. Curving wall is clad in full-height maple paneling. Custom conference table resides at far end of room.

Below: Office. Within office adjacent to principal office, bowed wall translates outward curve of principal office's oval plan. Inlaid maple paneling covers built-in credenza along exterior window wall.

FORUM AT PARK LANE

Dallas, Texas
1989

Familiarity means everything to a senior citizen moving to a retirement village, an event typically marked by disruption and loss. The retiree's morale can be difficult to sustain, let alone boost, but the design of the Forum at Park Lane, a 310,000-square-foot retirement community that the firm completed in 1989, combines architectural tradition and currency to generate a sense of normalcy, sociability, and belonging.

The arrangements of the Forum at Park Lane resemble those of a country manor—a far cry from the harshly institutional profiles of many retirement complexes and an exquisitely accountable solution to the site parameters. The property, a long, narrow strip of land along Dallas's North Central Expressway, sits between an office park and a neighborhood of single-family houses, where covenants dictate strict height limits and setbacks. Four buildings—three apartment structures surrounding a central community center and dining hall—align along the site's major axis are joined by interior corridors. A health-care building sits just to the west of this row.

The apartment buildings' massing inscribes strong, regular rhythms along the street: Projected bays alternate with small, sheltered garden courtyards beneath a skyline of hipped roofs, gables, pediments, and sculptural chimneys. Cast-stone cornices and lintels brighten the red brick façades, and clearly organize the exterior in domestic proportions. Corridor volumes, resembling colonnaded loggias, support balustrades of stone piers and steel tracery. The massing of the 20,000-square-foot community building distinguishes it from the residential units—its H-shaped footprint encompasses a generous porte cochere with clustered columns at the entrance and a broad, bowed bay facing a patio and fountain at the rear.

The health-care building divides into three levels; each provides a distinct level of service, from intermediate care to skilled nursing. Such smooth transitions become imperative in the ecology of retirement communities, both materially and conceptually, to ensure continuity for resident seniors in a place they can easily recognize.

Site plan

1. Club building
2. Residential building
3. Healthcare building

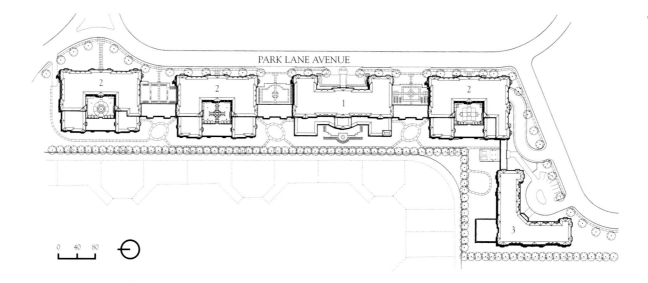

PARK LANE AVENUE

0   40   80

Opposite top: Park Lane Avenue Façades. Massing of buildings form series of connected "manor houses" at scale that gives clear identity to residential and community structures and anticipates relationship with future low-rise office development across the street.

Opposite bottom: Clubhouse Dining Room. Community center's massing and fenestration express double-height volume of main dining room at center of courtyard elevation.

Top: One-story Link Building. Single-story interior corridor structures connect all buildings on site. Plan arranges single-loaded line of apartments at rear of corridors.

Bottom: Chimney at typical apartment house. Decorative brickwork and cast stone copings accentuate each chimney mass.

Top: Pergola in Apartment Courtyard. Domed pergola set upon Tuscan columns animates garden in apartment courtyard.

Bottom: Typical Apartment Courtyard. Pilaster-framed porches mark courtyard façade of each residential building. Massing at termini of complex steps down in scale from three stories to one story.

PRIVATE APARTMENT RESIDENCE

1990

The firm designed this 4,500-square-foot apartment and some of its custom furniture for a businessman as if to substantiate a series of vivid daydreams. Disparate material elements marshal themselves into a sensible yet whimsical narrative order distinguished by exceptional craftsmanship.

At the entrance hall, the front door opens into a skylit, octagonal tower of rough-faced Indian Baruli Red sandstone enclosing a foyer floor patterned in granite tile that repeats the tower's octagonal geometry. As the tower's shaft rises dramatically three stories through the space, its lower-level portals resound in upper-level window openings that take in circumferential light, visually binding the apartment's multiple levels.

The lower level orients chiefly southward, with extended terraces on the southeast and southwest affording marvelous views. The foyer opens into a sparely furnished central loggia defined at either end by heavy, folding forged-iron gates wrought in original patterns, with abstracted animal heads (reminiscent of Doric bucrania) and simple wave and dart tracery. The loggia leads on the west side to a formal dining room with a custom-designed dining table, and also to a catering kitchen and bathroom. On the east, the loggia flows into a living room and adjacent personal kitchen, the latter tiled in a granite checkerboard pattern. The kitchen's architecture relates directly to that of the living room. The two spaces divide across a counter, and the massing of the solid stainless-steel kitchen cabinets and appliances—designed as furniture—steps back toward the center to deepen the space with hushed reflections from the living room's vantage.

The main stair of maple risers and treads wraps around the sandstone tower and leads to a central study on the upper level. This dusky, luxuriant space radiates warmth under gabled ceilings, with integral Arts and Crafts–inspired shelves, cabinets, and furniture milled from jarrah, a dense, reddish-brown wood of Australian origin. To the west of the study lie guest quarters within a two-story subvolume: a guest bedroom, a bath, and a kitchen that connects—via a circular stair detailed in stainless-steel railings—to an open loft at the mezzanine level (which holds a separate sitting area plus copious storage, reached by an upper stair with treads of fine stainless-steel grating).

The master bedroom, bathroom, and sitting area occupy the east side of the upper level. Built-in furniture divides the space beneath the rib vaults of the master bedroom. A bed in the center backs up to a massive headboard sculpted in figured maple and other woods as a cluster of skyscrapers, juxtaposed against a cloudscape painted onto the sky-blue ceiling. On the opposite side of the headboard, a credenza and cabinets form a dressing area. To the rear of the bedroom lies a small sitting room The pièce de résistance of this apartment is its escapist master bathroom. In the foreground are a shower and deeply sunken granite tub within a glass enclosure limned in polished stainless steel. A miniature stone bridge steps over the sunken tub from the bath area to the powder room, where a white-lacquered wood vanity sits in a niche beneath a frieze of white, gray, and black marble—a secluded, restful spot to end the journey through the apartment's several idealized worlds.

North-south Section

1. Entry
2. Foyer
3. Loggia
4. Study
5. Master Bath
6. Sitting
7. Storage

Opposite: Sandstone Tower with Skylight. Indian Baruli Red sandstone tower rises three stories beneath skylight at center of penthouse apartment, anchoring organization of spaces on horizontal and vertical axis.

Top left: Entrance Hall. Art Deco console sits within a niche of entrance foyer at base of stone tower. Octagonal floor patterns are rendered in granite.

Bottom left: Stair to Sitting Room. Stainless-steel stair wraps around upper circumference of stone tower. Treads of stair resemble finely machined sidewalk grating material.

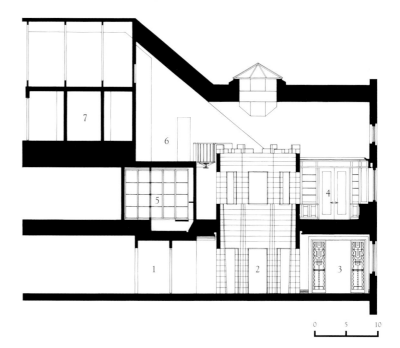

Loft plan

1. Sitting room
2. Guest sitting room
3. Storage

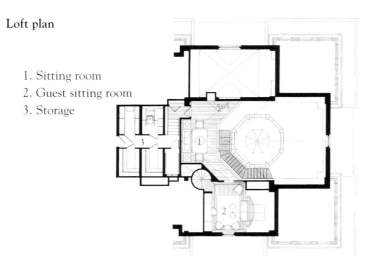

Upper plan

1. Study
2. Master bedroom
3. Sitting room
4. Master bathroom
5. Powder room
6. Guest suite
7. Terrace

Lower plan

1. Foyer
2. Loggia
3. Living room
4. Dining room
5. Owner's kitchen
6. Party kitchen
7. Guest suite entry
8. Terrace

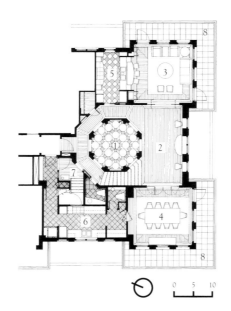

0   5   10

Opposite, top and middle:
Loggia. Formal loggia forms east-west axis with dining room and living room, between forged-iron-and-glass gates that fold to enclose it at either end.

Opposite, bottom: Loggia. Loggia opens into living room on east side of apartment, past folding gates. Furniture and lighting of several periods follow a French Deco aesthetic.

Top left: Guest Bedroom. Loft of guest sitting area overlooks guest bedroom (with kitchenette to rear) on west side of apartment. Art Deco wall sconces highlight bowed balcony.

Top right: Master Bedroom. Freestanding skyscraper sculpture of figured maple, lacewood, and pomele mahogany divides room and serves as bed console. Vaulted ceilings are painted sky-blue with clouds.

Bottom: Master Dresser. Dressing-area side of sculptural room partition contains mirror, counter, and cabinets. Clock-tower cabinet plays starkly against celestial ceiling mural.

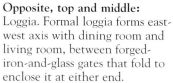

Opposite, top: Kitchen. Stainless-steel cabinets and appliances (*left*) with granite countertops bow outward gently from rear kitchen wall. At *right*, vertical massing of steel cabinets in owner's kitchen pushes backward above sink to extend volume of combined kitchen and living room across a medial counter.

Opposite, bottom left: Study. Sandstone tower (foreground) interlocks with and opens into Arts and Crafts–style study in view taken prior to furniture installation.

Opposite, bottom right: Study. Floor, shelves, cabinets, and furniture in study are fabricated from jarrah, an Australian wood colored a deep reddish-brown.

Top: Master Bathroom. Suite encompasses tub and shower enclosure of glass and polished stainless steel with walls of white marble. White-lacquered wood vanity at rear sits beneath frieze of steer heads in white, gray, and black marble.

Bottom left: Sitting Room. Chrome-and-leather seating area upon antique Navajo rug overlooks apartment from mezzanine level.

Bottom right: Guest Sitting Room. Dormer window in gabled roof pours daylight into mezzanine-level guest-sitting-room loft.

1201 F STREET

Washington, D.C.
1990

In downtown Washington, where rigid height limits make for squat office buildings, the vertical presence of 1201 F Street NW is striking. This 230,000-square-foot office building resides in an old retail district that has lost more than half its historic architecture to late-20th-century office development. Thus it follows the tradition of the relatively few prewar structures that remain— e.g., the Woodward and Lothrop department store two blocks east—but in a contemporary way.

This building speaks with subtle Viennese inflections to those mostly straight Neo-Classical forebears, as is evident in its bluntly expressive hierarchy of layered cubes and simplified, abstracted ornament. Tripartite organization divides the building's façades both horizontally into a strong base, shaft, and top, and vertically into two prominent towers bracketing a set-back central volume. The corner juncture of bays curves outward slightly as an overture to the street. (A distinct two-story retail volume joins the building's southwest corner).

The façade's potent detailing begins at street level, where wainscoting of Canadian green granite anchors the two-story limestone base. Pilasters surround retail storefronts and begin the building's rise toward the sky. About the F Street entrance, the pilasters culminate as piers of staggered heights—a pair of brass eagles rests upon the two central piers surrounding the entrance. The building's lift continues in the elegantly detailed shaft, which varies between the tight stone patterns of the lateral towers and the more open alignments of the central elevation's tile-like masonry, which holds cast-stone sills, lintels atop recessed brackets, and brass squares set into the brick at regular intervals corresponding to windowsills and lintels. The façade's solid masonry surface yields to the restrained fenestration of muntined windows engraved across it. The building looks tall, owing to the windows' cadence, which pulls the eye upward toward the top.

Beneath the major upper cornice, a row of stone brackets holding granite-and-brass medallions culminates the base and shaft's chromatic details. Above this cornice, the central mass terraces back 20 feet at the 11th floor, where a stone trellis opens the solid definition of the shaft edge and spans the width between the towers, revealing crowns of layered planes that form interlocking cubes, a heroic restatement of the building's basic geometry.

The erectness of the massing recurs in the office lobby, the building's chief public space, where a double-height central space has one-story alcoves flanking it to the east and west. A dark, rich palette of stone and wood intensifies the depth of the lobby. The floor's light-and-dark grid of Spanish Emperador marble grounds the dark wainscoting of the same material, beneath panels in three varieties of anigre. The dimensions of the plastered ceiling coffers directly reflect the grid of the marble floor, as if to summarize—conceptually, at least— the building's skyward reach.

Opposite: Southeast Corner, 12th and F Streets NW. Massing of 1201 F Street divides into two-story base, eight-story shaft, and two-story cap. South and east facades have pairs of projecting bays bracketing shallow setback of central volume. Roofline embellishments link corner towers. Twenty-foot setback at upper two floors fortifies the presence of masonry façade below it. Stone, granite, and brass façade details grow more complicated in progression toward the building's top.

Above left: Entrance Detail. Metal-and-glass canopy marks recessed main entrance to office lobby. Flagpoles and eagles punctuate third-floor setback, with brass details that relate to brass insets of brickwork, which, in turn, relate to brass elements of two-story building cap, visually binding the building's base, middle, and top.

Lobby-level plan

1. Main lobby
2. Garage elevator lobby
3. Elevator lobby
4. Retail space
5. Garage entry

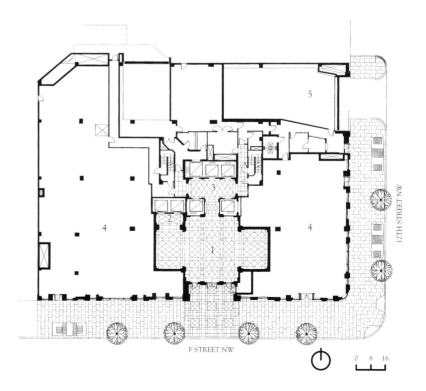

Left: Eleventh-Floor Setback Detail. The building's midsection sets back above 10th floor to define tower tops and provide exterior balcony for 11th-floor tenants. Ornamented, stylized brackets articulate the setback below a thin, projecting cornice line, with a stone trellis above. Note syncopated rhythms of narrow and wide trellis members. The two wider posts sheathe steel-cord members of Vierendeel trusses, which structurally support setback without the need for separate, continuous column line.

Below: View from Southwest. This view shows the "niche" building between 1201 F Street and the historic Homer Building. By agreement among adjacent property owners, 1201 F Street was required to set back 20 feet from the Homer Building's east façade above the second floor. Rather than have this two-story portion look like a mere extrusion of the base, as is common in post-1950s Washington buildings, the firm elected to have this façade portion read as a separate "out parcel."

Right: Main Lobby. This axial view looks from the central entrance doors through the two-story main lobby space, past an intermediate vestibule and into the elevator lobby beyond. One of two second-floor balconies lies behind frosted-glass parapet.

Below: Main Lobby. This view of the main lobby looks toward guard's desk and east alcove beyond. Lobby finishes include Emperador Light and Dark marble floors and wainscot; three different varieties of figured anigre on paneled walls; and coffered, veneer-plastered drywall ceilings. Panel profiles were inspired by the works of Josef Hoffmann.

PRIVATE RESIDENCE

Maryland

1991

This client visited Tuscany and photographed numerous villas in that region to prepare the firm for the design of a 10,000-square-foot house in a hilly, wooded neighborhood near the Potomac River northwest of Washington, D.C. The house holds the client's large collection of art and wood furniture, and supplies generous spaces for entertaining on the first floor in addition to the second floor's commodious private living quarters.

Several formal strategies validate the design's Tuscan inspiration—its symmetrical massing, minimal punched fenestration within stucco wall surfaces, and a low-pitched hipped roof of slate with broad eaves atop decorative brackets boxed in at the roof-wall junction. Yet, its details are quite stylized. The footprint forms a basic L-shape, the cardinal corner of which steps back as a flat plane holding the deeply recessed entrance between two angled wings that read as lateral towers. Battered bays center these projecting volumes at the ground level to pull the eye upward, a vertical orientation augmented by tall, narrow openings of doors and muntined windows defined by limestone surrounds and lintels. This house's vertical aspect interplays with the limestone base and bands of cast stone between the first and second levels, which emphasize its horizontality. A large loggia occupies the far end of the northern wing; the southern wing conceals a garage well away from the main entrance and patio areas.

The siting of the house speaks directly to the landscape. On the rear façade, the wings of the house stretch out to embrace the deep, formal lawn that reaches out to the forest beyond it. At the center of the rear façade, a glass curtain wall extends between the two wings beneath a master-bedroom terrace. This curtain wall contains a strong white grid of mullions and muntins that contrasts with the black framing of the windows around it and bolsters the house's dynamic interplay of horizontal and vertical elements.

Four columns mark the edges of the formal entrance foyer—like the columns throughout the house, they are oval rather than round. The first-floor rooms organize along a gallery that extends north-south and terminates at circular vestibules. On the south, this hallway leads to the dining room, and, beyond it, a galley and abundantly daylit contemporary kitchen, with a breakfast room at the rear. On the north, a smaller frontal corridor leads to an intimate library, two bathrooms, and a bar area just inside the loggia. At the center of the first floor, a family room, rear center hall, and formal living room range along the curtain-wall façade looking onto the lawn—an outdoor extension of these indoor spaces. The stair hall, tucked inside the core of the house in front of the living room, leads to the suite containing the master bedroom, dressing room, and bathroom on the north; a central volume containing offices; and children's bedrooms on the south.

The spaces on both levels of the house flow together mellifluously. Individual components of the interior maintain an airy, open atmosphere, yet manage to seem sufficiently secluded to afford privacy, the sum of which attests to the firm's fluency in adapting historic period styles to contemporary conditions.

Site plan

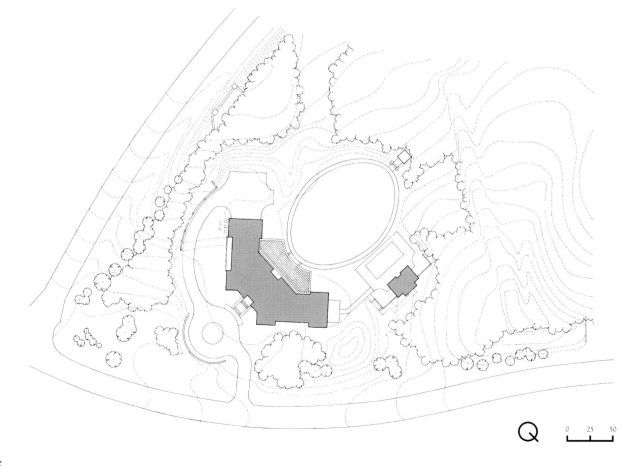

Opposite: View of Entrance Façade. The entrance façade is angled both to contain the entry court visually and to draw the eye toward the deeply recessed entrance.

Opposite, top left: View Along South Elevation. Along the south façade, the heavily massed corners bracket the kitchen's glass curtain wall.

Opposite, top right: Rear Patio Area. The living and family rooms align within glassed-in area along the rear patio. The master bedroom suite opens out onto a roof deck at the second floor.

Opposite, bottom: Loggia and Rear Façade. Spacious loggia adjoins rear patio areas, affording views to lawn and garden areas beyond it, and provides shaded outdoor space during summer months.

Right: Detail of Glass Wall Along Rear of House. The interplay of horizontal and verticals develops further in the composition at glass wall of main living areas. Strong vertical emphasis of paired oval columns and second-floor window openings contrasts with horizontal subdivisions of glass curtain wall, which are painted white to differentiate them from vertically emphasized window openings.

Below: Rear Façade During Evening. When daylight fades, rear glass wall offers dramatic transparency between indoors and outdoors.

Northwest elevation

0 5 10

Southeast elevation

Southeast elevation

First-floor plan

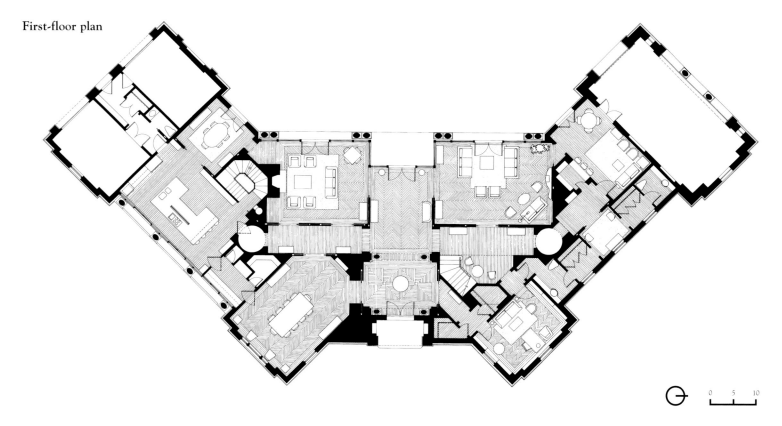

0 5 10

Right: Kitchen. Stained wood floors and cabinets provide warmth and contrast to the white-painted curtain wall, which floods this spacious room with daylight.

Below: Family Room. Living and entertaining spaces stretch along the curtain wall of glass, which spans across rear of house and adjoins large outdoor patio areas to provide expansive views of lawn and wooded edges.

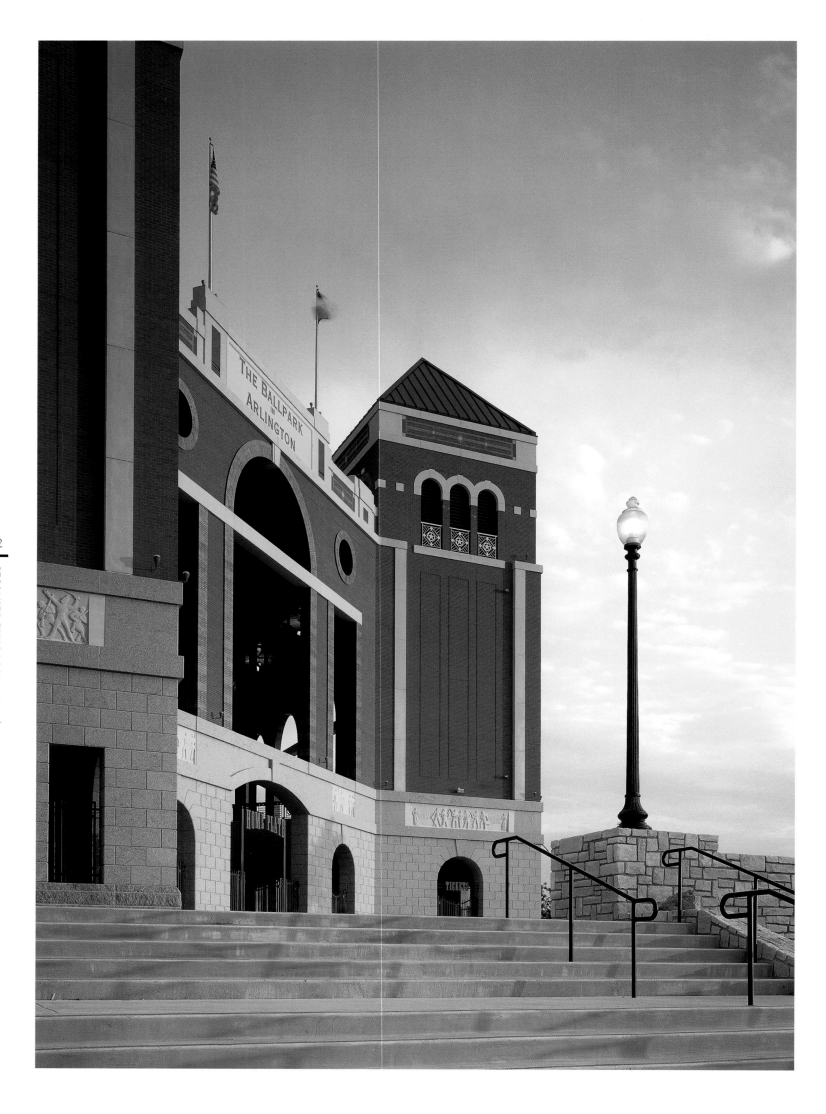

THE BALLPARK IN ARLINGTON

Arlington, Texas

1991

Before ground ever broke for The Ballpark in Arlington, the owners of the Texas Rangers stipulated that baseball fans everywhere should see their new stadium on television and "recognize this as Texas." How could the fans not? Nearly every aspect of this 49,200-seat stadium dedicates itself to the land of lone stars and steers. The park also exclusively celebrates baseball, a sport in which the notion of place (for example, Chicago's Wrigley Field) means the world. At least, it did until about the 1960s, when the convertible designs of football/baseball stadiums turned ugly and gave both games short shrift. The stadium that the firm completed for the Rangers' 1994 opening day will forever be known as one of the first of a new generation of modern buildings to restore the eminence of the baseball field to baseball dreams.

The firm had not designed a ballpark before beating 16 other architectural firms in the Rangers' 1991 design competition. But if it seemed a dark-horse entrant, it won the job by virtue of its extensive research into the history of ballparks, baseball lore, and Texan history, which translated into the most thorough vision for the ballpark. The firm also developed a coherent urban design for the 320-acre property where this ballpark would sit.

Most major-league stadiums occupy dense city centers, but the Arlington site, along the southern edge of Interstate 30 between Dallas and Fort Worth, seemed barren by comparison, with scarce architectural bearings to offer design guidance. The firm, therefore, created a new context in its master plan, imagining an urban future for the site where the stadium

Opposite: Detail at Home Plate Gate. Matching stair towers flank each of four main gates. Here, Home Plate Gate serves as Ballpark's main ceremonial entrance—and most convenient for arrival from the northwest, with ticket booths at base of far tower.

Right, top: View from Nolan Ryan Expressway. Each of four façades is articulated with major and minor towers to syncopate arch rhythms. Major stair towers terminate each façade, flanking principal entrances. Ceremonial Home Plate Gate stands at center of image.

Right, bottom: Site Plan. Competition site plan shows Ballpark's position in part of 320-acre masterplanned site, landscaped with pathways and trees amid commercial, retail, and residential development.

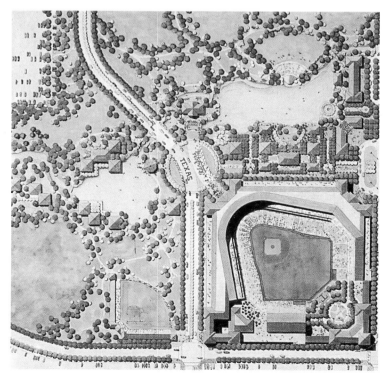

Opposite, top: Ballpark Way Façade. Typical walls comprise granite base of smaller entrance arches at pedestrian scale beneath larger brick arches emphasizing Ballpark's monumentality. In this image, curtain wall fills arches across office-building portions of perimeter.

Opposite, bottom: Office Building Entrance. Lone-star and baseball iconography ornament metal-and-glass canopy at office-building entrance. Bas-relief friezes on spandrel panels depict events in Texas and baseball history.

Below: Aerial View. Opening-day aerial shot of Ballpark from northwest reveals orthogonal concourse building wrapping seating bowl, with Home Run Porch at right field. Entrances between corner stair towers correspond to infield base positions for easy orientation and wayfinding.

could preside over a youth ballpark, a Sports Hall of Fame, an amphitheater, 500,000 square feet of retail space, and commercial and residential development arrayed around a 12-acre pair of lakes created from Johnson Creek, which bisects the site near Arlington's Convention Center. The firm also served as landscape design architect.

Among the masterstrokes that give the building its civic character are the pairs of pyramid-roofed stair towers flanking each corner of the complex, which identify themselves, for easy orientation, by their respective relationships to the infield—the main entrance at the northwest corner being Home Plate. The Ballpark's square outer massing reconciles the irregular geometry of the bowl with the orthogonal lines of the surrounding roads. On

the approach to any of the Ballpark's 810-foot-long façades of brick and Texas Sunset Red granite, it has the attitude of a monumental civic building, though the architect made its scale humanly tractable by breaking each elevation into a base, body, and parapet. Sixteen-foot-high arcades, further gauged to pedestrian proportions, range along the full lengths on all sides of the granite base; each arch holds a pair of seven-foot iron gates whose catenary upper profiles hang in shallow counterpoint to the arches' curves. Between the base and body, bas-relief friezes depict significant scenes from the history of both Texas and baseball. The body of the façade would become a colossal expanse of brick but for generous 75-foot-high arched openings, each the width of two smaller lower arches, with

Roof plan

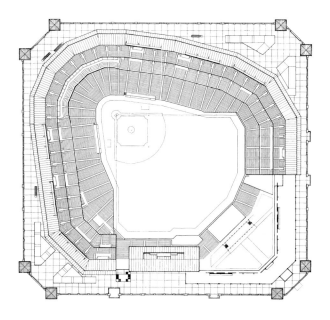

Club concourse plan

1. Club concourse
2. Home Run Porch—
   upper concourse
3. Learning Center
4. Learning Center
   auditorium
5. Concessions
6. Offices
7. Bullpen Bar
8. Ballroom/Diamond
   Club
9. Bullpen Lounge
10. Press box

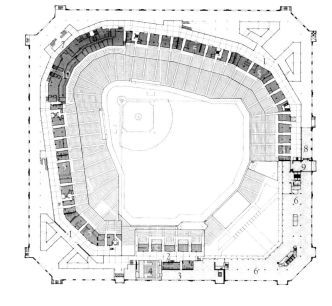

Main concourse plan

1. Main concourse
2. Concessions
3. Walk of Fame
4. Tickets
5. Suite lobby
6. Stadium Club entrance
7. Visitors' bullpen
8. Commercial/retail
9. Office Lobby
10. Learning Center lobby
11. Texas Rangers' bullpen
12. Hall of Fame
13. Sports Grill lobby

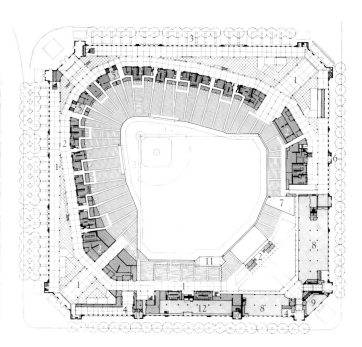

Site plan

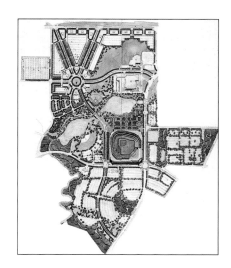

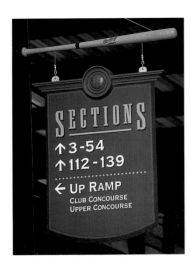

Far left: Directional Signage. Baseball bats and assorted sports imagery transforms wayfinding graphics into ornament.

Left: Detail at Suite Entrance. Murals based on Hall of Fame photographs identify each pair of suite entries.

Below left: Lower Deck Main Concourse. Main concourse serving the lower deck divides into outer concourse (shown) following orthogonal outer geometry and inner concourse lined with services.

Below right: Detail at Lower Deck Vomitory. Graphics identify sections above vomitories and add ornament throughout concourse, reinforcing traditional themes. Structural X-braces (foreground) fuse at circular gusset plates.

Opposite, top: Upper Deck Concourse. Exterior parapet wall along upper deck concourse holds baseball light fixtures.

Opposite, bottom left: Seating Detail. Aisle-seat stanchions incorporate cast lone-star logo of Texas Rangers.

Opposite, bottom right: Diamond Stadium Club. Terraced seating in Diamond Stadium Club at left-field corner of club level maximizes number of tables with views to field.

polychrome brick surrounds and bright keystones; the band of cast stone crossing the façade at the spring line of the larger arches; and full-height brick-and-cast-stone piers marking the distance along the façade's length. Beneath the double white lines of the parapet, lone-star medallions hang between the arches; atop the parapet, lamps rendered as baseballs punctuate the skyline.

The first steps to the stadium's interior are awesome ones. Through the heavy arches, the main concourse, wrapping nearly all of the perimeter, soars to 70 feet upon colonnades of green structural steel, each supporting a truss with a lone-star medallion at the center. Stone and stucco surfaces soften the light across large wall planes. Concession stands and restrooms present themselves conspicuously near each entrance. Two corners contain triangular, structural-steel ramps to the upper levels that give sweeping views into the concourse and its gigantic structural-steel X-bracing, as well as to the outer landscape. A dramatic escalator at the Home Plate entrance looks like a pair of crossed baseball bats. These vertical circulation routes, along with interior stairs, lead to a club concourse at mid-building height, and lead further upward to a bright, broad upper concourse on the roof, with shaded pavilions atop it.

The southeast entrance behind center field, however, is different, because this quadrant of the perimeter is a 140,000-square-foot, curtain-walled office building four stories high, marked by a canopy, and housing the Legends of the

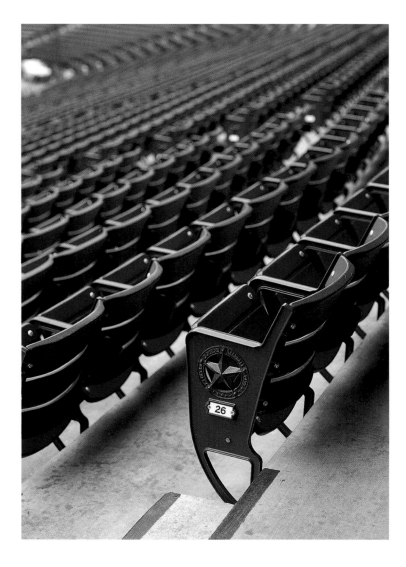

Opposite: View Down First-Base Line. At right-field corner, typical seating bowl arrangement stops at Home Run Porch (at right). Gap between discontinuous sections reveals unique view down the first-base line toward home plate. Rail design incorporates Texas lone star.

Above: View from Office. Center-field office building serves multiple purposes: It controls center-field view from home plate and blocks wind's effect on long fly balls. Offices also prove to be coveted real estate, increasing value of facility. Shown are Rangers' executive offices toward left-field corner.

Below left: View from Suite. Glass line of suites recesses behind suite seats and over-hanging level. Suites' interiors hold amenities and finishes commensurate with their status.

Below right: Press Box Detail. Several rows of club seats continue downward in front of press-box windows to aid visual transition among seating levels from afar and on television.

Game museum, the Rangers' organization and club, and a 300-seat auditorium. Already, this office complex indicates the activity to come with the planned commercial development—there are people coming and going around the building even during the off-season.

That Center Field entrance leads beneath the office building to a festive plaza of retail and concession stands above the bleachers. In the economics of modern baseball, a team cannot sustain itself without specific income streams, and the firm designed the Ballpark to maximize them for the Rangers. The calculus of seating arrangements represents as much a new economic model of the sport as anything, by placing a critical mass of high-dollar seats close to the infield to boost ticket revenue. The stadium has three basic seating tiers: lower, club, and upper deck, positioned for equitable sight lines, with certain sections near the foul poles rotated slightly toward home plate to ease viewing. Two levels of luxury suites occupy spaces behind sliding glass doors above and below the club tier. The main press box sits discreetly behind home plate. And in a landscape without external landmarks, the Ballpark holds its own on the interior—Home Run Porch, behind right field, perches two larger tiers of seats beneath a lofty canopy, recalling old Tiger Stadium in Detroit. All of the Ballpark's numerous innovative amenities train toward one thing: the field, an asymmetrical lawn whose bowl sinks 22 feet below grade, where the game begins.

Home Run Porch section

1. Main concourse
2. Hall of Fame
3. Learning Center auditorium
4. Home Run Porch upper concourse
5. Sports Grill
6. Concession

Typical section

1. Main concourse
2. Mezzanine
3. Lower suite
4. Club concourse
5. Upper suite
6. Upper concourse
7. Concessions

Opposite: Center Field Office Building. Rooftop advertising panels double as supplementary wind-control devices atop office-building portion of concourse perimeter, whose curtain wall is detailed in white steel trusswork.

Below: Home Run Porch. Seating areas throughout Ballpark were given special identities to increase seats' value. Design of Home Run Porch refers to old Tiger Stadium, transforming what would be otherwise ordinary bleacher seats into magnet section for season-ticket holders.

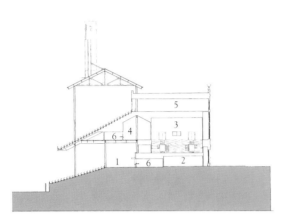

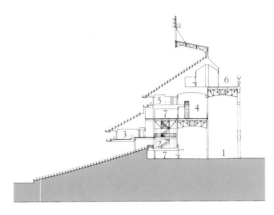

DR. PEPPER YOUTH BALLPARK

Arlington, Texas
1991

Opposite, top: View of Stands from Left Field. Stands of Dr. Pepper Youth Ballpark visually link to main Ballpark at Arlington (at rear) and hold 750 fixed seats beneath stylized vernacular shed extending from first to third bases. Steel members at either end of stands form Texas lone-star pattern and provide wind bracing.

Opposite, bottom: View of Stands Toward Center Field. Steel trusswork repeats patterns found at main Ballpark at Arlington, including star medallion behind home plate.

Below left: View Toward Major-League Ballpark. The major-league park is visible from the Youth Ballpark's concourse. Edge trusses of the concourse's shed roof make references to that of major-league park's Upper Deck canopy.

Below right: Concourse View. A single concourse wraps around stands at ground level beneath shed roof structure and underside of seating risers. Concessions, restrooms, clubhouses, and other support spaces are placed beneath seating. Trusses similar to those of major-league park support perimeter of shed roof. Main Ballpark is visible in background.

Among the major highlights of the firm's master plan for the Ballpark at Arlington is the Dr. Pepper Youth Ballpark, funded as part of the Ballpark bond referendum and programmed to engage the community beyond major-league game events by hosting the games of the region's youth leagues.

The Youth Ballpark sits on the site northwest of the larger facility and, like that park, incorporates stylized elements of the Texas vernacular, though scaled to dimensions appropriate to young people. It seats 2,000 people—750 of them in fixed seating on risers beneath a steel pavilion, which resembles an open shed, centered behind home plate and extended out to first and third bases. Additional berm seating is available in the outfield areas. The steel trusswork echoes that of the main Ballpark, particularly the edge trusses along the outer perimeter, and each end of the pavilion holds a full-height steel star that acts as wind bracing and provides a visual link back to the Rangers' park.

A single concourse runs along the outside of the youth park beneath the shed roof structure and the underside of the seating risers, and provides broad views to the Ballpark in Arlington's stately arches and brick walls. A concession stand, clubhouses, and restrooms lie beneath the seating off of the concourse.

The Rangers' organization administers the Youth Ballpark, which is active at all hours of the day from April through October. Given the professional atmosphere of the youth park, it seems entirely likely that some young pitcher or shortstop will find inspiration to advance to the major leagues.

SANGER LOFTS

Fort Worth, Texas
1991

Any attempt to revitalize historic city centers like that of Fort Worth hinges on getting people to live downtown again, but, because people want to live in contemporary comfort, this prerogative often conflicts with preservation goals. The central question becomes one of how to furnish up-to-date housing without destroying historic buildings. One possible and quite convincing answer appears in the Sanger Lofts, where the firm's adaptive redesign of the 1929 Sanger Brothers Department store building, originally designed by Wyatt C. Hedrick on a site fronting West Fourth Street between Houston and Throckmorton Streets, observes both the past and the present without compromising either period.

The firm restored the exterior of the five-story stone-clad building according to the exacting historic-preservation guidelines set forth by the U.S. Department of Interior. The design adds a sixth-floor penthouse, but sets it back from the ornately dressed parapet far enough to hide it from the street and create deep, private outdoor terraces. The rooftop cooling tower remains exposed as a tribute to the building's status as the first building west of the Mississippi River to have air conditioning.

On the interiors, the greatest handicap to residential reuse was the potential darkness of their 52-foot depth. The redesign opened up most of the 59 loft interiors into unobstructed plans with 8-foot-high windows, which bring daylight into the 13-foot-high spaces and create a sense of placid expansiveness and monumentality. As a respite from this openness, sleeping areas lift three feet off the floor behind parapet walls for privacy.

The interiors continue to recite the building's historic narrative in old maple floors, which received light sanding and refinishing. Newly inserted mechanical ducts, light fixtures, and sprinkler pipes are left visible within living spaces to strengthen their loft character. Exposure of $2\frac{1}{2}$-foot-thick interior columns with sleek conical capitals keeps the building's architectonic elements intact.

The firm also left in place the Sanger building's internal connection to the adjacent Fakes Building to the north and carved out six large loft units within the Fakes structure. Thus the Sanger Lofts project satisfies urban priorities as well as domestic needs, by looking beyond an individual property to the significance of the block as a unit of city-building.

Opposite: Apartment Building Lobby. Walls and floors of Sanger Lofts lobby are more highly finished than those of apartments, yet reflect the building's loft character in open ceilings above cornice molding and exposed, black-painted pipes and ducts. Custom-designed wallpaper frieze features stylized steer head.

Right: Exterior Façade. Not seen in this view, significantly, is new top level of penthouse apartments above original roof line, behind tall, historic parapet. Spaces between parapet and penthouses form private urban courtyards. Façade restoration follows Department of Interior Guidelines for Historic Preservation.

Far Right: Living Room. Open kitchens, dining, and living areas share light from 8-foot perimeter windows.

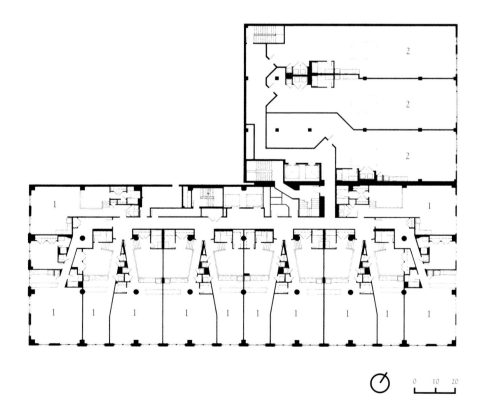

Typical floor plan

1. One-bedroom apartment
2. Residential loft space

Opposite, left: Typical Apartment. Walls behind kitchen enclose elevated bedroom behind open parapet wall, which admits light into deepest reaches of bedroom space. Elevation of bedroom blocks living-room sight lines. Conically capped columns express original building structure and reinforce loft aesthetic.

Opposite, right: Raised Bedroom. Bedrooms open to light of perimeter windows. Thirteen-foot-high ceilings allow raising of bedroom platform by several feet to provide privacy.

Right and far right: Loft and penthouse Apartments. Eight-foot-high windows flood apartments with light. Intact original wood floors and flared columns, along with exposed ductwork, typify lofts' character.

Penthouse floor plan

1. Apartment
2. Private roof terrace
3. Community roof terrace

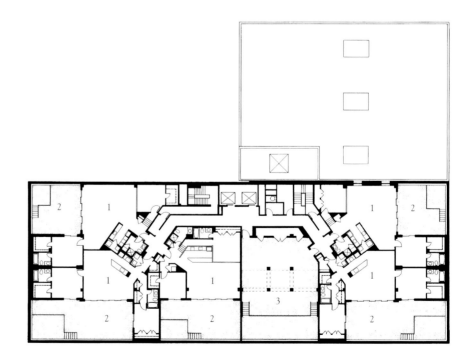

FORT WORTH CENTRAL LIBRARY

Fort Worth, Texas

1992

Build it and they will read. So ends the bittersweet saga surrounding the Fort Worth Central Library, which opened in 1901 as the Carnegie Public Library of Fort Worth inside a Beaux-Arts temple. The city demolished that building, and for numerous political and economic reasons, in 1978 the library opened a new building that lay completely underground beneath two square blocks, with Lamar Street running over it. By the early '90s, the below-grade building had developed more than 300 leaks. In 1992, the library hired the firm to design a two-story shell atop the existing library both to stop the leaks and create more space for future expansion. The library didn't have adequate funding for interiors, but figured the arrival of the shell in 1995 would help ignite fundraising. It did, and in 1999, the library dedicated its 50,000-square-foot interior expansion in a restorative act of civic faith. The temple is back, and it is filling up with books.

The simplified Neo-Classical building's exterior honors the Carnegie original with a larger-scale reinterpretation of its massing: The main (south) façade measures 460 feet long, broken into three parts. The entry pavilion's grand pediment, supported by a cleanly detailed entablature upon two pairs of Corinthian columns, centers squarely upon Lamar Street to form a new terminus. Beyond this pilastered pavilion, two two-story wings run out to either side, articulated around small courtyards.

The recessed entrance leads to a grand sequence of crisp lobby spaces—bright and elegantly spare—whose details match those of the façade. The circulation desk sits immediately inside on the east. The lobby's axes cross beneath a quiet rotunda; to the west are the 20,000-square-foot youth library (the courtyard of which holds a children's reading garden), the youth activity space, the media library and stacks, audio-visual rooms, and staff work areas, with computer workstations throughout. To the east, the design transforms the library's former entrance lobby into a deep art gallery leading downstairs to the library's general collection within the existing volume.

In that gallery, bronze stair-rail panels depict an open book. Numerous pieces of furniture that the firm designed for the library become functional art objects, such as the suspension-bridge computer stations in the youth library. The thoughtful simplicity of the design accounts for the tightly margined economies of the library's funding yet ensures the institution's permanence. It revives the more glorious days of the institution's past and vouches for its future with tremendous optimism.

Opposite, top: South Façade. Lamar Street, which formerly passed over below-grade library, now ends at new Neo-Classical entry pavilion beneath pedimented volume to left.

Opposite, bottom: Main Entrance. Simplified Neo-Classical elements articulate the minimally fenestrated north façade, behind which lie reading rooms, lobby, and nonpublic spaces.

Right: North Façade Detail.

Left: Grand Entrance Lobby Details. Spandrels of second-floor openings hold open-book and pen ornament to represent reading and writing.

Below: Grand Entrance Lobby. Design of lobby relates to that of pedimented entrance of exterior, with similar large columns at central corners. Floor and wainscot are honed and flame-finished French Corton limestone.

Elevation

Ground-floor plan

1. Grand entry lobby
2. Lobby
3. Youth library
4. Youth activity space
5. Media stacks
6. Media library—public area
7. Gallery
8. Circulation
9. Peter Rabbit's Garden

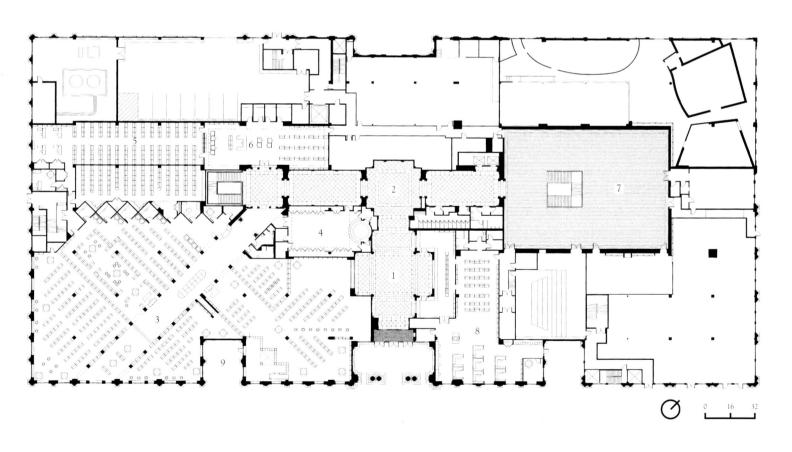

Opposite: East, West, and Central Lobbies. Major circulation path connects grand entry lobby to open stairs on east and west.

Right: Two-story Rotunda. Central lobby, where grand entry lobby meets east and west lobbies, connects to second floor via circular opening.

Below right: Stair Detail. Bronze railings frame cast-bronze panels with open-book design at stairways connecting first-floor and basement-level collections.

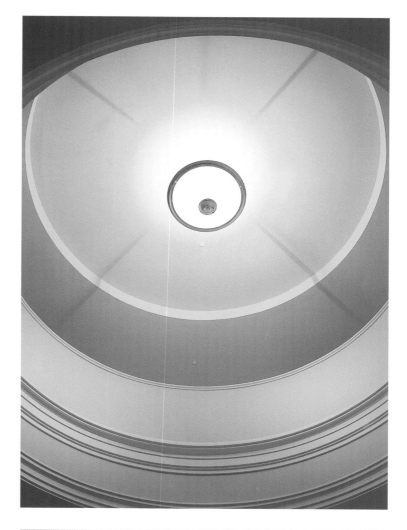

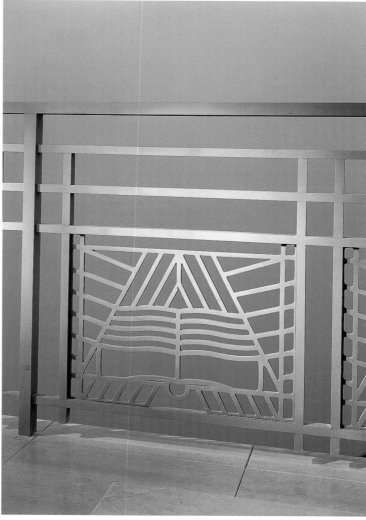

The Amon G. Carter Multi-Media Center

Opposite: Entrance to Amon G. Carter Multi-media Center. Typical entrance to specialized collection shows refined proportions of Classical columns and entablature meeting lines of modern butt-glazed glass doorways.

Right: Entrance to Hazel Harvey Peace Youth Center. Rainbow archway marks entrance to youth center. Through arch lies main circulation path cutting diagonally through youth center, which contains computer work area and public-access computer terminals.

Below left: Computer Table in Peace Youth Center. This computer table in youth center is designed as suspension bridge between skyscraper towers. Its central location makes it equally accessible to all age groups and easy to supervise.

Below right: Public-access Catalog Stations in Peace Youth Center. Tall booths with peaked roofs hold public-access computer stations, making them easy to find and providing some user privacy.

117

SUNDANCE EAST

Fort Worth, Texas
1993

In downtown Fort Worth, this 102,000-square-foot complex fills a square block with a multiplex cinema, a bookstore, restaurants, and office space two blocks east of Sundance Square and directly north of the firm's Nancy Lee and Perry R. Bass Performance Hall (pages 144–157). Sundance East's low-scaled architecture re-energizes the block with shopping and entertainment to complement the residential and cultural activity that has recently returned to the district's streets.

Anchoring the project is the nine-screen AMC Palace Cinema, which totals 41,000 square feet. The cinema sits behind an asymmetrical Art Moderne façade that links it spiritedly with the Art Deco facade of the Sundance West

AMC cinema two blocks away and also raises the memory of downtown's original Palace movie house, which served the area until the 1960s. The arrangement of the cinema interior allows single projection rooms to serve multiple theaters, most of which include deep stadium-style seating for dramatic viewing closer to the screens.

Just west of the cinema, on the northwest corner, stands the three-story Barnes and Noble Bookstore (with its double-height interior entry rotunda), which rounds the corner in a white Streamline wrapper with horizontal strip windows that negotiate between the cinema façade and the brick volume on the southwest corner holding the bookstore's café. The two-story brick structure, finessed with simple bands of polychrome

masonry patterns, posits two cubes converging upon a cylindrical corner tower with an octagonal cone roof.

East of the brick corner, the stuccoed south façade sits directly across the street from Bass Performance Hall, for which it serves as a Neo-Secessionist set piece, with graphic details painted across its surface, a course of ceramic tiles just beneath the parapet, and ornamental grilles emphasizing the proportions of the windows. This section steps back from the street slightly, forming a restaurant courtyard facing the performance hall. Finally, a two-story brick storefront completes the southeast corner of the block with details evolved from Texas vernacular. The composition artfully augments the variety of vintage commercial architecture around Sundance Square.

Opposite: Cinema Façade and Marquee. Tower sign announces cinema complex for several blocks. Art Moderne design references Art Deco Sundance West cinema two blocks away. Outsized movie posters classic to Fort Worth punctuate upper portion of façade, with smaller posters of current features at eye level.

Ground-floor plan

1. Cinema entry
2. Grand stair
3. Office lobby
4. Projection mezzanine
5. Cinema below
6. Bookstore
7. Café
8. Nightclub entry
9. Restaurant

Upper-floor plan

1. Cinema entry
2. Grand stair
3. Upper concessions lobby
4. Lobby
5. Cinema
6. Bookstore

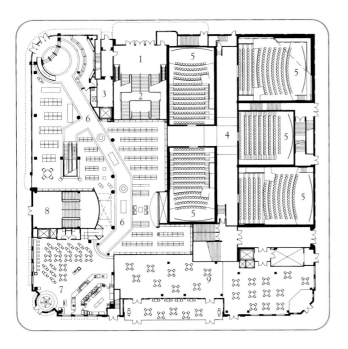

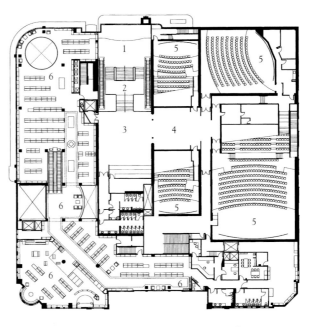

  0 8 16

Left: Retail Entrance. Corner entrance improves visibility of retail storefront in Streamline volume. Bookstore occupies first and second levels, with offices on third level.

Below: North Entrance to Retail Building. Circular opening between bookstore floors announces to shoppers the upper level's presence and restates curved corner of exterior.

Right: Bookstore Café. This café is finished with an open ceiling, hanging low-voltage light fixtures, and stained concrete floor, in contrast to bookstore beyond, framed by paired columns and detailed entablature.

Below: Southwest Retail Entrance. Brick building at southwest corner foils stucco façades on either side yet maintains street's proportions and rhythms.

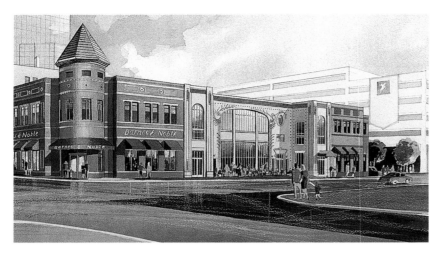

Below: Angeluna Restaurant. Recessed restaurant entrance creates outdoor dining room with views directly across street to Bass Performance Hall. Upper and lower windows join in common frame to create grand gesture toward the Hall. Expressive fenestration, blue ceramic tile, and painted vines enliven stucco façade.

WELLS FARGO BUILDING

Fort Worth, Texas
1993

Floor plan

1. Office lobby
2. Retail space
3. Restaurant
4. Kitchen
5. Dining patio

Opposite: West Elevation. Horizontal façade subdivides into subtle changes in plane to emphasize vertical proportions of building. Color changes and belt courses clearly articulate composition of base, middle, and capital.

Above: Entrance Lobby. Elegant entrance lobby, through glazed portal, holds marble floors and Tuscan columns.

In Fort Worth's historic Sundance Square district, the firm designed the Wells Fargo Building in 1993 to engage the street and strengthen the neighborhood's pedestrian scale and rhythm. The building stands five stories above Main Street, but a number of traditional visual strategies break down its mass and make it seem familiar to its urban context.

The composition of the façades divides vertically along stonelike belt courses into a base, middle, and capital—the lighter surfaces of the base and capital contrast with the middle section's masonrylike panels and curtain wall. Across its length, the façade articulates into oriel windows whose volumes hold ornamental railings, solid tower forms with punched windows, and glass curtain-wall bays. This dynamic yet harmonious ensemble of colors and textures emphasizes the vertical dimension of the horizontal building.

Through the slick, butt-glazed entrance lies the main lobby, with a marble floor and the quiet dignity of Tuscan columns. On the south side of the building's storefront base lies a small courtyard that serves as an outdoor dining patio for the ground-level restaurant, further animating the building's base with the life of the street.

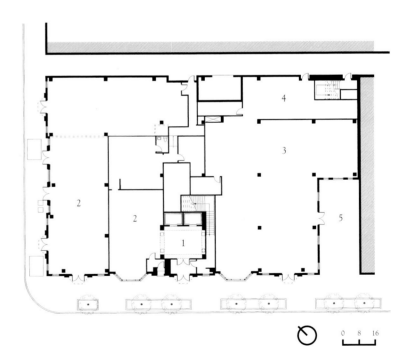

0   8   16

WORTHINGTON HOTEL

Fort Worth, Texas
1994

The Worthington Hotel, a 1980 building that the firm restored to four-star status in 1997, envelops its guests in a regional, contemporary Classicism that consistently reminds them that they have landed in historic downtown Fort Worth rather than in any of the anonymous interiors that typify modern hotels. The 504-room hotel required complete upgrades of its electrical and mechanical systems to meet building codes, and public spaces and guest rooms needed modernization to make them competitive among travelers.

Guests encounter the hotel's local spirit the moment they enter the airy, double-height lobby, where the marble floor gives way to carpet bearing the lone star of Texas—the star repeats in accent-lighting fixtures.

A double stair, newly installed during renovation, leads to the Grand Ballroom level. The stair and a large balcony cantilevered atop columns both have medium-stained cherry stile-and-rail raised panels on them, matching the finish of columns, door frames, pediments, and arches throughout the public areas. Dining-room booths sit within niches that form between piers and pilasters connected by beams and detailed in an Arts and Crafts idiom. From the balcony hang acorn pendants that represent the Texas live oak. Throughout the hotel appears the head of a Texas steer—in the frieze motifs of guest rooms, and even the restaurant's china (pages 134–135)—giving the hotel's amenities a sense of thoughtfully planned completeness.

Opposite: Reception Lobby. Renovation added raised cherry paneling, custom carpet designs, new lighting, and new furnishings. Finials below balcony panels refer to Texas live oak.

Right: Reception Desk Detail. Transaction counter surfaces are marble and brass. Typical writing surface at standard height lifts out to accommodate guests or employees using wheelchairs. Steer-head design on brass inset resembles that found throughout hotel's décor.

Ballroom section

1. Vehicular drop-off
2. Entry hall
3. Grand stair
4. Ballroom/meeting rooms
5. Exhibition hall
6. Parking ramps
7. Garage
8. Main entry
9. Ballroom pre-function
10. Grand ballroom
11. Projection booth
12. Corridor
13. Meeting room
14. Mechanical room

Opposite: Conference Center Entry Hall. Renovation added double stair giving direct access from street-level arrival lobby to Grand Ballroom complex above.

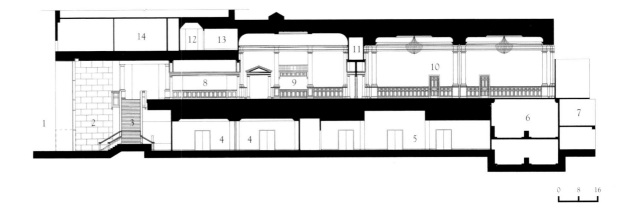

Ballroom plan

1. Entry hall
   (one level below)
2. Grand stair
3. Executive conference room
4. Meeting room
5. Meeting room pre-function
6. Ballroom pre-function
7. Grand ballroom
8. Bar
9. Storage/prep area
10. Stair to classrooms

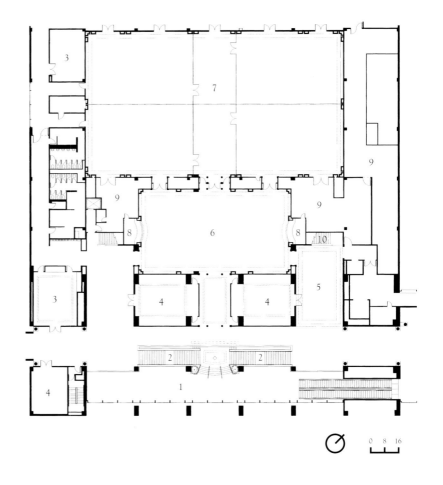

DAVID M. SCHWARZ/ARCHITECTURAL SERVICES

Left: Grill Entrance and Reception Area. Hostess/cashier desk has raised wood paneling and tapering piers at each corner. Lantern-topped piers connect with beams. Ceramic-tile floor's cruciform and stripe patterns relate to china design.

Below left: Star of Texas Grill. The Grill has two dining rooms, one with open seating and another (shown) with booths that have high backs for privacy. Piers, pilasters, and beams enclose booths as intimate spaces.

Below: Typical Room Before Renovation. Guest rooms formerly lacked character, with generic furnishings.

Below right: Typical Corridor Before Renovation. Corridor extended 300 feet as a mostly bare expanse. Finishes were plain, abstract, and without distinction.

Bottom: Typical Renovated Room. New furnishings and fabrics give rooms a regional sense. Custom-designed wallpaper frieze incorporates steer-head motif. Many new furniture pieces are of custom design and construction, with medium-stained cherrywood.

Right: Typical Corridor After Renovation. Redesigned corridors remain same length as before renovation, but broad vertical stripes of wallpaper de-emphasize their length. Alternating wall sconces modulate frequency of visual events along corridor. Ceiling-mounted light globes mark wide entry recesses and reduce contrast between entry areas and corridor lengths.

Far left: Entrance to Pre-Function Room. Barrel-vaulted corridor at top of Grand Stair serves as elegant entry to pre-function room and passage to Grand Ballroom beyond. The corridor passes between two large meeting rooms separating pre-function room from pedestrian traffic on the bridge.

Left: Pre-Function Room Detail.

Below: Pre-Function Room. This space stands centrally between Grand Ballroom and four large meeting rooms on the same level, and a ring of break-out rooms on level above, at top of stairways at either end.

Opposite: Grand Ballroom. Wood paneling, pilasters, ceiling coffers, and chain-hung lighting creates refined atmosphere. This large room subdivides by means of walls that fold into concealed pockets between pilasters.

DAVID M. SCHWARZ/ARCHITECTURAL SERVICES

OBJECTS

The firm's redesign of the Worthington Hotel in 1994 involved the creation of individual china patterns for each of four levels of guest food service. The patterns were also carried by Barneys New York, Neiman Marcus, and a number of boutique shops. Each porcelain setting relates to the firm's architectural motifs in that it takes inspiration from local and regional iconography, stylized in simple, elegant patterns.

The Worthington Stencil pattern, which the firm designed in five-piece typical settings for the hotel's grille, renders an abstracted longhorn steer head in black, platinum, or gold on white porcelain—the same stencil pattern as that of guest-room friezes. The geometric figures in black, platinum, or gold on the Deco Lines pattern capture the spirit of Texas Deco architecture.

The Sanger Frieze pattern adapts the details of steer heads and lone stars from the frieze of the Sanger Lofts building the firm converted in downtown Fort Worth (pages 106–109). The repeating pattern appears in shades of gray around the plate's full circumference with highlights of bright red bands. The Sundance pattern, in gold and royal blue, also has steer heads lining the four poles of the plate's perimeter, with a delicate medallion at the center.

Opposite: Typical Setting. This five-piece place setting combines Worthington Stencil and Deco Lines patterns designed for Worthington Hotel in Fort Worth, Texas. The two patterns were intended to coordinate. Worthington Stencil has stylized figures of steer heads, a pattern derived from stencil pattern on guest-room friezes. Deco Lines recalls Texas Deco architecture. Both patterns were produced in black, gold, or platinum on white porcelain.

Below: Sanger Frieze. Cup and saucer pattern is inspired by steer and star details of Sanger Lofts building in downtown Fort Worth.

Right, clockwise from top left: Dinner Plates. Sanger Frieze, used for room service; Worthington Stencil (in gold), a special run made for the hotel's owners; Deco Lines (in black) produced for Barneys in New York; and the Sundance pattern, used for the hotel's top-tier restaurant.

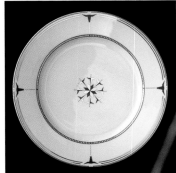
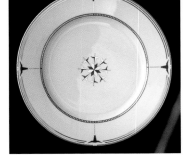

FURNITURE

As part of several architectural commissions, the firm has designed numerous pieces of custom furniture. Alongside the fixed elements of their respective project interiors, the furniture's fine detailing, rich materials, and a high level of craft create comprehensive environments, often combining regional imagery with exotic influences.

Materials vary to suit the sensibility of each project, ranging from hardwoods in traditional settings to metal and glass in more contemporary spaces. For one client, the firm designed several quite different furniture pieces tailored to specific design themes: An Art Deco–inspired pedestal table seats six but folds to form a half-oval upon a pedestal built of a light-colored hardwood stylized with botanical patterns; the

top consists of a hardwood veneer with delicate marquetry. A dining table for 12 and a buffet, made of solid American black cherry with fiddle-back moave veneer have native plant patterns in marquetry of light maple with darker geometric inlay—atop the buffet floats a three-part glass top to protect the wood finish from hot items. In a separate furniture suite for this client, the Arts and Crafts style influenced by Greene and Greene predominates: A sofa built into surrounding casework, wood-framed club chairs, a desk, and a coffee table are all built of Jarrah, a dense, reddish-brown Australian hardwood. This client's eclectic tastes prompted the firm also to design a medicine cabinet and stool in stainless steel and glass with custom hardware.

For another residential interior, the firm designed a dining-room buffet and table of Honduras mahogany, a sustainably harvested species endorsed by the Forest Stewardship Council. These pieces, too, are of Arts and Crafts inspiration, with simple lines and demure hardware details that emphasize the master craftsmanship in their construction. This same client also commissioned four pieces of furniture that extend the American Rustic style as practiced by the Reverend Ben Davis.

Two designs for desks and a conference table arose from the firm's commercial office projects. Their wood patterns, inlaid marquetry, and, in the case of the conference table, a sculptural base merge gracefully with their surroundings to emphasize the exacting quality of the firm's vision in pursuits of any scope and scale.

Opposite, right, and below right: Dining Buffet. Built in same materials and manner as dining table, buffet measures 21 inches deep and 93 inches long. Height matches that of dining table at 30 inches. Top and front incorporate stylized marquetry of native grass in light maple with inlays of bubinga and ebony. Solid members consist of American black cherry with primary veneer of fiddle-back moave. Three-part glass riser raises top height to 34 inches upon silver-leaf pyramids and protects wood finish from hot items. Base contains drawers and cabinets lined with silver cloth. All hardware is of custom design.

Far right: Master Bathroom Cabinet and Stool. Freestanding medicine cabinet for master bathroom consists of stainless steel with exposed fasteners. This two-part piece has a tall cabinet with small niches and adjustable glass shelves upon a granite-topped base that doubles as a towel rack. Accompanying stool has black leather top.

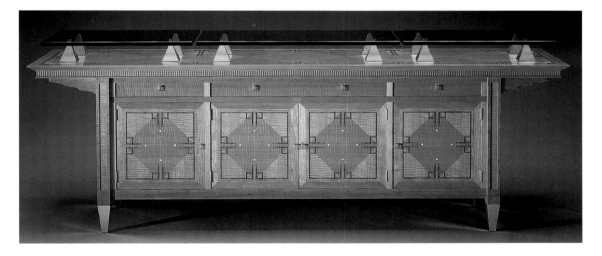

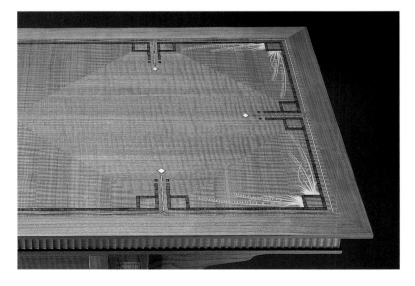

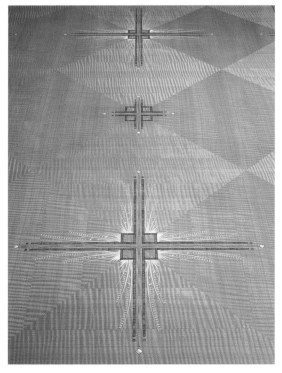

Above: Dining Table. This table for formal dining room measures 46 inches wide and 107 inches long and seats 12. Table top (*left*) has a geometric veneer design in light maple with Bubinga and ebony inlay. Marquetry is a stylized representation of native grass. Solid wood is American black cherry with fiddle-back moave as veneer.

Right, below, and bottom: Loggia Table. This table for entrance loggia is patterned after Art Deco pedestal tables. In closed position, the table forms a half-oval against a wall. Table expands to full oval form upon custom-fabricated hinges and devices that re-center the top over the base. Pedestal of solid makore has hand-carved design of native grass. Top is veneer makore with grass marquetry in Goncalo Alvez.

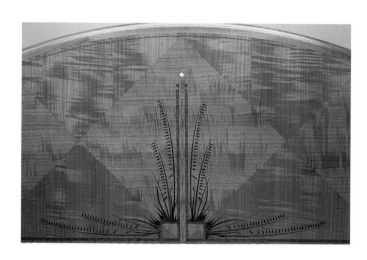

DAVID M. SCHWARZ/ARCHITECTURAL SERVICES

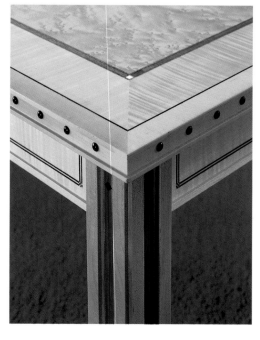

Above: Conference Table. Bird's-eye maple tabletop has inlaid marquetry on pedestal base of maple, stainless steel, and granite.

Far Left: Tabletop Detail. Round conference tabletop shows radial, book-matched, bird's-eye maple veneer with inlay pattern of ebony, mahogany, mother of pearl, and sterling silver.

Left: Desk Detail. Juncture of tabletop, apron, and leg shows various inlaid motifs. Materials and details derive from those employed in architectural woodwork throughout the interior.

Right and below: Desk. Figures of pommele sapeli form quiet diamond book-matched patterns atop this desk, within inlaid bands of curly maple, and details of mother-of-pearl, silver, and dyed pearwood surrounded by solid mahogany. The desk measures 84 inches long by 36 inches deep by 30 inches high. The legs have bands of dyed pearwood atop chrome feet.

Right: Dining Room China Cabinet. This Arts and Crafts china cabinet was designed to hold decorative dinnerware and pottery in its upper glass-framed cabinets with flatware and serving pieces in the lower drawers and cabinets. It measures 102 inches high, 65 inches wide, and 22 inches deep, and consists of Honduras mahogany with hardwood pegs and fittings.

Below: Buffet Detail. The solid mahogany buffet has stylized floral inlay on its front, dovetailed drawers, pegged mortise-and-tenon joinery, and bronze butt hinges.

Bottom: Dining-Room Buffet. This Arts and Crafts buffet designed to hold flatware, linens, and centerpieces is 36 inches high by 100 inches wide by 22 inches deep. Its details derive from Greene and Greene. It consists of certified Honduras mahogany with hardwood pegs and fittings and has a heat-resistant top of Rojo Alicante marble.

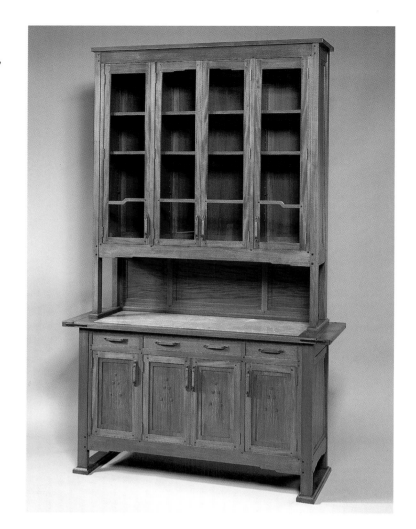

Top: Dresser. This 10-drawer, two-cabinet dresser of American black cherry with figured moave veneer reinterprets American Rustic furniture designs, with raised applique and pole trim along base.

Above, right and left: Headboard/Dresser. Articulated dresser with 24 drawers doubles as padded-leather headboard on opposite side. Its geometric poletrim details complete a contemporary rendering of American Rustic furniture, which, by nature, is defined by its imprecision.

Left: Buffet with Armoire at Rear. Low cabinet and 9-foot armoire decorated with laureltwig appliqué designed as site-specific furniture of American Rustic derivation.

NANCY LEE AND PERRY R. BASS PERFORMANCE HALL

Fort Worth, Texas
1996

The Nancy Lee and Perry R. Bass Performance Hall, which opened in May 1998, represents downtown Fort Worth's crowning cultural achievement, an embodiment of the highest aspirations that the firm, working with the board of directors, set forth for the physical and spiritual renewal of the city's historic Sundance Square district. The building houses the Fort Worth Symphony, the Fort Worth Opera, the Fort Worth Dallas Ballet, the Casa Mañana Musical Theater, and the quadrennial Van Cliburn competition, and it also hosts traveling Broadway shows as part of its wide range of artistic offerings.

Bass Performance Hall's form resolves a complex set of inquiries involving the nature of its urban environment, the honored tradition of grand performance spaces, and the collective pride of civic assembly, and it transcends those concerns with a bold assertion that human creativity is divine: Two 48-foot-high limestone angels, the work of sculptor Marton Varo, emerge from the main façade with gold trumpets.

Whereas the firm designed nearly all of its other projects in the Sundance neighborhood to blend in seamlessly with the district's extant fabric, the Bass Performance Hall purposefully stands out in a skin of Texas Cordova Cream limestone—not common downtown—to call attention to its special purpose. The firm conceived Bass Performance Hall as an opera house; nearly every specification observes the history and ritual of artistic performance as canonized by opera houses such as La Scala in Milan, the Garnier in Paris, and the Magyar Allami in Budapest—though it judiciously adapts these precedents rather than repeat them verbatim. The language of its massing, fenestration, balconies, trellis, sculpture, and entrance canopy evolves out of the Secession, and, by extension, the Classical Revival period, to reflect periods of great intellectual curiosity and accomplishment—times when, not coincidentally, many of the works performed in the hall were first produced.

The hall's configuration responds succinctly to both exterior and interior imperatives, balancing the limits of a 200-by-200-foot block with the need to seat up to 2,056 audience members comfortably. The central auditorium has support volumes flanking it symmetrically in transepts on the east and west and ceremonious public spaces within the formal entrance-lobby volume on the north. (The backstage area stands merely a wall away from the southern property line, and the last row of seats are only an exit corridor away from the northern boundary.) Setbacks diminish the building's apparent bulk, articulating the corner entries, central lobbies, and the stage house as distinct volumes from the auditorium, enhancing the structure's human scale but maintaining its grandeur.

The relationship of the hall's various parts creates the sense of formal progression as one approaches and enters the building. Entry foyers in the form of quartered octagons

Opposite: Street Level View of North Façade. Bass Performance Hall's main façade faces Fourth Street with 48-foot-high limestone angels on either side of windows into the orchestra and mezzanine grand lobbies. Massing revives classic precedents of European opera houses. Gradual setbacks establish human proportions yet emphasize the hall's grandeur. Details reinterpret Secessionist and Classical Revival patterns of ornament.

Right: Sketch of façade detail.

Opposite, top: Rendering. Watercolor rendering of north elevation shows relationship of central auditorium volume to corner entrance foyers and transepts at rear housing support functions.

Opposite, bottom: Overall View at Twilight. Each of two main entrance foyers stand at northern corners (northwest entrance is shown) to receive pedestrians and create clear views within large lobbies. Copper quarter-domed roofs express volume of foyers within and presage the domed ceiling of Founders Concert Theater.

Below right: Angel Sculptures at Twilight. Limestone angels bearing gold-leafed trumpets appear to emerge from stone walls of north façade, as viewed from main corner entries.

stand at the northeast and northwest corners beneath two-tiered, quarter-dome roofs clad in copper, whose shapes foretell the great dome of the auditorium and visually buttress the grand lobby and transept volumes. The foyer volumes, dressed with pilasters, recessed limestone panels, and large square and small oval windows framed in French limestone, open to pedestrians beneath opulent steel-and-glass canopies.

Inside the corner entries, the foyer spaces soar 70 feet high. Pilasters around their perimeters —detailed, like the columns in the grand lobby, in a stylized Classical order specifically for Bass Hall—launch complex vaulted ceilings painted with native Texan botanical patterns that give way to soft cloudscapes.

The corner entrances create a clear view between them through the orchestra grand

lobby, which runs east-west along Fourth Street. Northern light plays gently onto the aluminum-leafed columns, cabled balcony railings, custom lanterns, and Italian Fior di Pesca marble floors and wainscoting of the two-story grand lobby through four tall, narrow windows; these windows correspond with arched windows above a small terrace outside the two-story lobby stacked atop the grand lobby at the mezzanine level. Interpenetrating sight lines join these multiple lobby levels, visually engaging patrons among all levels.

The hall itself assumes a horseshoe shape for an intimate, elegant viewing and listening environment. Aligning balcony parapets form a ground court, with a forestage zone leading to the stage and its 40-foot-high proscenium. There are five levels of seating: the

orchestra level with surrounding parterre seats; the box tier with 21 boxes each seating six to eight people; the mezzanine; and the upper and lower galleries. The interior, enveloped by the sconce-lined stacks of balcony fronts, culminates in a great coffered, domed ceiling that is painted, like the foyers, with cloudscapes. The curvature and rib placements of this dome diffuse sound to prevent unwanted focusing.

The hall's acoustical shell was engineered to accommodate symphony, opera, and Broadway productions variously without undermining the quality of any of them. The versatility of Bass Performance Hall promotes its purpose as venue for many types of performance, a guarantee that it will serve as a truly populist cultural asset to all the people of Fort Worth.

Preceding pages: West Grand Foyer Floor. View from upper-most overlook at gallery level shows spiral pattern of Italian Fior di Pesca marble floor radiating from grand stair to west entrance portal.

Top far left: Detail of West Grand Foyer Dome. Two-tiered domes crown each of two grand foyers. Murals on lower portions of domes depict Texas flora, and give way to cloudscape murals above them. West grand foyer (shown) displays evening sky.

Top left: East Grand Foyer Dome. Murals on east grand foyer dome depict sky at dawn.

Bottom: West Grand Foyer. Multi-story grand foyers at east and west entrances link all front-of-house levels with a series of overlooks. West grand foyer (shown) serves as main entrance point from Sundance Square neighborhood of downtown Fort Worth.

Right: Donor Wall. Donor-recognition panels of carved glass sit atop marble monolith on granite bases. Center glass panels of donor-recognition walls have carved angel motif drawn from limestone sculptures on front façade.

Below: Orchestra Level Grand Lobby. Two-story grand lobby links two entrance foyers at orchestra level. Grand lobby is part of modulated series of front-of-house spaces creating a ceremonial progression from entrances to main auditorium.

Above left: Detail at Grand Foyer Overlook. At mezzanine grand lobby level, overlooks provide views into east grand foyer, serving as popular perches from which to watch crowds during intermissions.

Above right: Detail at Mezzanine Grand Lobby. Pilasters and ceiling vaults line mezzanine grand lobby.

Left: Detail at East Grand Foyer. Box-tier-level overlook shows pilasters in "Bass Hall Order" and bracketed custom light fixtures.

Opposite: Richardson Room. The space serves as a lounge for founding patrons before performances and during intermissions. This room also provides a flexible function space either by itself or combined with the adjacent Green Room.

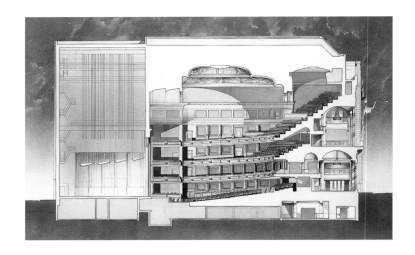

Left: South-north section through auditorium.

Opposite: Stage in Symphonic Mode. Variable acoustical features create multipurpose venue within Bass Peformance Hall. In this view, orchestra shell tower and ceiling reflectors deploy for optimum reverberation in the symphonic mode.

Lower-gallery plan

1. Gallery promenade
2. Gallery bar
3. Lower gallery
4. Upper piano box
5. Main stair
6. Catering
7. Fly gallery

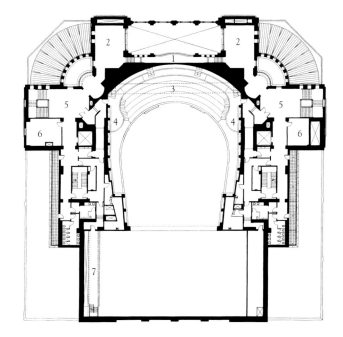

Orchestra-level plan

1. Orchestra grand lobby
2. Parterre seating
3. East corner entrance lobby
4. Gift shop
5. Loading dock
6. Orchestra seating
7. Stage
8. Star dressing room
9. Stage door
10. Box office
11. Ticket lobby
12. West corner entrance lobby

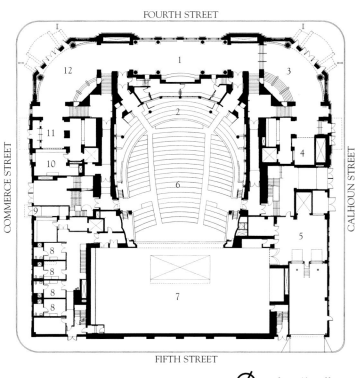

FOURTH STREET

COMMERCE STREET

CALHOUN STREET

FIFTH STREET

Above left: Founders Concert Theater. Box tier provides 21 boxes, each seating six to eight patrons. Each box has private anteroom also serving as a sound and light lock.

Above right: Founders Concert Theater. View from mezzanine side box.

Left: Detail of Founders Concert Theater. View toward house-left side of proscenium from orchestra parterre. Forestage and actors' boxes sit just left of proscenium edge.

Opposite: Founders Concert Theater. Named the Founders Concert Theater in honor of founding patrons, this concert hall seats 2,056 audience members in intimate, elegant room. Classic horseshoe opera-house plan ensures excellent sight lines. Large ceiling dome and light fixture center the space.

MADDOX-MUSE CENTER

Fort Worth, Texas

1997

Opposite left: North Façade. The north façade of Van Cliburn Recital Hall distinguishes itself with its large arched window between a red granite base and red-brick, Flemish-bond body with a polychromatic tile frieze.

Below: Street View of Northwest Corner. Historic former City-County Hospital building (far left, at northeast corner) becomes part of Maddox-Muse Center and sets dimensions for its design, which simulates urban block of small-scale structures. From center to right: Van Cliburn Recital Hall, the central mechanical plant, and McNair Rehearsal Studio.

The Maddox-Muse Center, designed in 1997 and completed in 2001, stands in downtown Fort Worth as a study in elegant urban variation. The firm's design for this complex of recital, rehearsal, and support spaces fills three-quarters of the 40,000-square-foot block directly east of the Nancy Lee and Perry R. Bass Performance Hall in downtown Fort Worth. It turns one contiguous structure into four distinct buildings, and retroactively gives each its own character—the firm designed each segment of the block as if it had been built in a different era from the others.

One of the components in this assemblage, the former City-County Hospital building at the block's northeastern

corner, is indeed historic, dating to 1913. Now renovated, it houses the offices of Performing Arts Fort Worth and allied arts groups. The relatively modest scale and simple detailing of this building inspired the firm's design for the balance of the site.

The historic building's west wall meets the complex's newly constructed portions within a curtain-wall-enclosed atrium of industrial specifications—hard masonry edges, exposed roof trusses, and light fixtures resembling shop lamps. The atrium serves as the Maddox-Muse Center's main entrance; its opposite side connects to the Van Cliburn Recital Hall, a crisply detailed cornerstone building that is strongly

Opposite, top: Street View of Southwest Corner. McNair Rehearsal Studio anchors southwest corner of site, clad in buff-colored brick with cast-stone bas-relief spandrel panels and frieze, and glazed-brick accents. Corner towers, pilasters, and bay windows break long façade into smaller parts.

Opposite, bottom left: "Central Plant" at West Façade. Central mechanical plant, at midblock of west elevation, stands between Van Cliburn Recital Hall and McNair Rehearsal Studio behind a façade of metal grids that suggests an industrial aesthetic. Loading dock opens to street level.

Opposite, bottom right: Detail of McNair Rehearsal Studio Bay Window.

Below right: Night View of Atrium. Minimalist industrial interior of main entrance atrium stands between historic hospital building (left) on the west and the Van Cliburn Recital Hall (right).

reminiscent of Louis Sullivan's National Farmer's Bank in Owatonna, Minnesota. It has a red granite base, a red-brick Flemish-bond-patterned façade embroidered with angel-feather patterns in polychromatic tile up two side towers and across the tile frieze, and a large, boldly arched window facing north. The west elevation of Van Cliburn Hall extends to the middle of the block, where it abuts the complex's central mechanical plant (also serving Bass Performance Hall), differentiated by its façade's industrial aesthetic of gridded metal cladding. The central plant elevation segues to the Art Deco–inspired façade of the McNair Rehearsal Studio, where the several shades of buff-colored brick have a rich, variegated cast, with colorful punctuation of glazed brick accents, and spandrel panels and a frieze of cast-stone bas relief.

Interior spaces of the Maddox-Muse Center connect internally to each other, and also to Bass Hall through a tunnel beneath Calhoun Street. The firm specified the Maddox-Muse interiors for maximum flexibility. Van Cliburn Hall's acoustical ceiling approximates the sound quality of Bass Performance Hall—fit for symphony rehearsals, but the space also may serve as a press room and overflow auditorium for the hall. Ballet groups rehearse inside the McNair studio, yet the space accommodates nearly all manner of performance as well as banquets and meetings. The sum of these interchangeable yet individuated parts augments the cultural wealth that Bass Performance Hall brings to Fort Worth and becomes an artistic asset to downtown in its own right.

Floor plan

1. Main entrance
2. Entry bridge
3. Canteen
4. Elevator lobby
5. Atrium
6. Van Cliburn Recital Hall
7. Lobby
8. McNair Rehearsal Studio
9. Ballet corps
10. Fifth Street entrance

FOURTH STREET

CALHOUN STREET

JONES STREET

FIFTH STREET

0   25   50

Opposite: Night View of Atrium Toward Main Entry. The curtain-wall-enclosed atrium encases the alley or "sideyard" with an industrial aesthetic between Van Cliburn Recital Hall and original Maddox-Muse Building. This space serves as the primary point of entry into the Maddox-Muse Center.

Right: Interior Northwest Elevation of Van Cliburn Recital Hall. The Van Cliburn Recital Hall is a multipurpose hall primarily intended for symphony rehearsals and recitals. Acoustical panels flip to allow for hard or soft acoustics or amplified performances. Aluminum tubular frame and perforated metal panels support and hide acoustical pyramids within ceiling, and also support technical lights and sprinkler fixtures. Natural light enters through large arched window to the north and two rectangular windows to the west.

Below right: Interior View of McNair Rehearsal Studio. This studio accommodates dance rehearsals and social gatherings. A fully sprung Maple dance floor covers the entire room. Acoustical draperies with blackout liners allow for audio visual presentations. Exposed ceiling, factory lighting, and large windows reinforce industrial aesthetic.

DISNEY'S WIDE WORLD OF SPORTS® COMPLEX

Walt Disney World® Resort
Lake Buena Vista, Florida

In the design of this 175-acre sports complex at the Walt Disney World® Resort, the master plan for the site places several major venues—a 7,500-seat Triple-A ballpark and spring training facility for the Atlanta Braves, a 34,000-square-foot field house, a tennis pavilion, and several additional venues accommodating more than 30 types of sport—around a system of green spaces, linking walkways, and a central square.

The architecture of the complex corresponds with the landscape design of subtropical vegetation shading the walkways, greens, and sheltered areas built into and around the venues. Landscape enhancements include street lighting, graphics, and ancillary buildings such as pavilions, refreshment stands, and rest rooms. The main walkway progresses north from the town square, placed approximately at the center of the site, to a stairway at the foot of the arcade fronts of the ballpark and field house, through which it continues around an allée of towering fan palms and terminates at an octagonal plaza.

The stadium and field house arcades stand 65 feet apart along the main walkway, carving a stuccoed streetscape in which periodic towers, following a pattern of setbacks, interrupt the arrangement's horizontal bias. The iron concourse gates of the stadium's arcade open to the main walkway, extending the promenade into the interior. Long solid expanses break down regularly in a rhythm of bays, doors, and windows, and graphic details become integral to the architecture to expedite the way through clearly organized interiors.

The tallest towers mark the main entrances of both structures. Octagonal tower tops repeat the geometry of clipped corner entrance façades and the entrance plaza. Concourses with stained-concrete floors, metal-clad sconces, and hanging lanterns lead to the deep bowl around the field of green Bermuda turf. Eighty percent of the seats run between first and third bases. There are two tiers of seats, and press rooms and four enclosed and two open-air suites stand at the back of the upper deck, above which runs a cantilevered trellis along its length. The field house's green tile roof rests upon painted gabled-arched steel trusses. The configuration of retractable seating stands converts easily to accommodate wrestling, martial arts, basketball, and in-line hockey.

Various surrounding venues are organized around a network of linear walkways, wherein landscape enhancements mark important intersections. Just outside the ballpark lie four professional fields and one infield for practice sessions. A world-class track-and-field facility incorporates a 0.7-mile cross-country track and grandstands for 2,000 fans. The Tennis Complex features 11 courts, with 1,162 seats around the center court. Outside the field house lie four fields suitable for soccer, football, or lacrosse.

Opposite: Axial View to South Along Main Walkway. The ballpark and field house façades frame and define this axis as the main pedestrian path of the sports complex.

Below: Site plan.

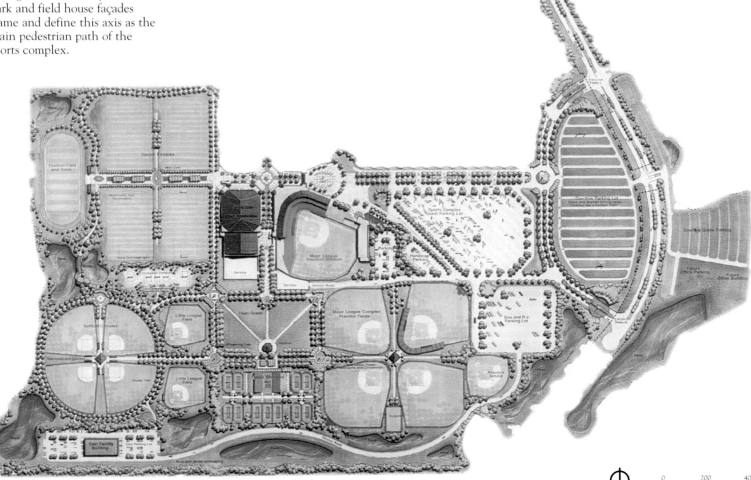

© Disney Enterprises, Inc.

Drawing by HHI, Inc.

0   200   400

Opposite: View Across Plaza to The Field House Main Entrance. Main entrances to the field house and ballpark open onto central plaza.

Below: The Field House Viewed From The Football Practice Field. Sports complex incorporates long vistas, such as this view toward the field house from the football fields.

East-west section

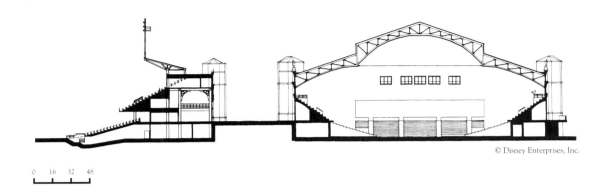

0 16 32 48

Roof plan

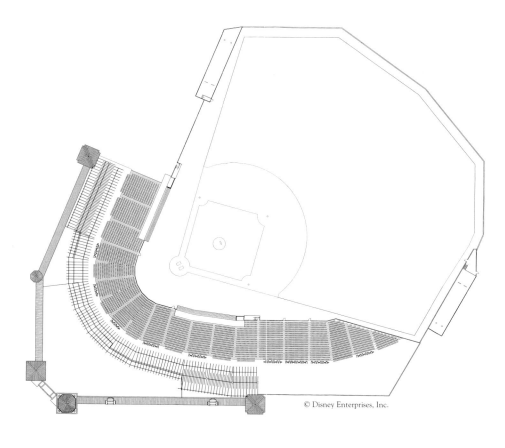

© Disney Enterprises, Inc.

Ground-floor plan

1. Home plate entrance
2. Concourse
3. Concession stand
4. Retail

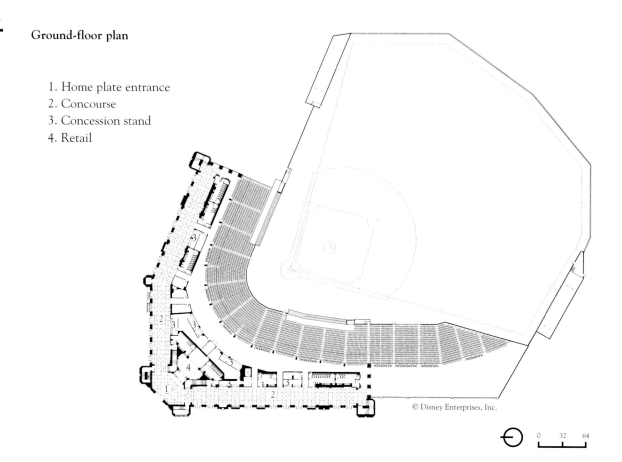

© Disney Enterprises, Inc.

0   32   64

Below: View Along The Field House Terrace. The field house terrace furnishes outdoor gathering space overlooking football practice fields.

Below: The Ballpark Main Concourse. Baseball-bat motif occurs along rail of upper concourse bridge.

Opposite: The Ballpark Upper Deck Seating. Cantilevered trellis shades spectators along parapet of upper deck.

SECTIONS **101** TO **112** SECTIONS **207** TO **220**

Concessions
Restrooms
Terrace

Restrooms
Terrace

Below: Ballpark Interior.
Eighty percent of the ballpark
seats align along infield areas.

Field house floor plan

1. Upper lobby
2. Concourse
3. Grand stair hall
4. Main court
5. Auxillary court

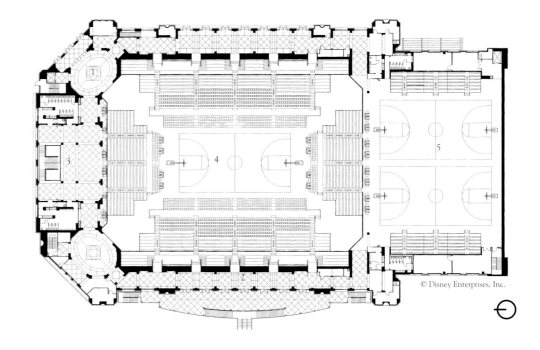

© Disney Enterprises, Inc.

Below: View of The Field House Arena. Painted gable-arch trusses define roof interior of the main field house arena. Fixed and retractable seating affords flexible configurations.

© Disney Enterprises, Inc.

Right: The Field House Concourse. Entrances to the field house seating bowl establish series of spaces defined by wide arched openings, ceiling treatments, and lighting.

Below: The Pavilion at The Tennis Courts. This pavilion comprises a series of pavilions connecting along colonnaded breezeways to enclose a central courtyard.

© Disney Enterprises, Inc.

© Disney Enterprises, Inc.

SEVERANCE HALL

Cleveland, Ohio

1998

Severance Hall, the historic home of the Cleveland Orchestra, holds a revered place in the annals of classical performance. Designed by the Cleveland firm of Walker and Weeks, this Neo-Classical landmark of Ohio sandstone and Indiana limestone opened in 1931 between Euclid Avenue and East Boulevard, on the campus of Case Western Reserve University. Musical Arts Association President John Long Severance built the hall as a gift to his wife, Elizabeth. Over the next six decades, however, as the orchestra accrued international esteem, it steadily outgrew the hall. Alterations compromised the building's ceremonial interiors, and dated technology limited its production potential. To complicate matters, the insertion of a new concert shell in 1958 by Music Director George Szell positively changed

Severance Hall's acoustical properties to the degree that some credited it for the Cleveland Orchestra's signature sound. But the shell's intervention entombed the hall's treasured 6,025-pipe, 94-rank Skinner pipe organ in a loft above the stage. By the 1970s, the organ was no longer in operation. Thus, in 1996, the Musical Arts Association commissioned the firm to reform the building in the spirit of Walker and Weeks—to correct past amendments to their design and build on its inherent vitality.

The firm devised a comprehensive scheme for Severance Hall, faithfully restoring 42,000 square feet of interiors and adapting 40,000 square feet to new uses while adding 39,000 square feet of newly constructed space. Exhuming the disused Skinner organ in

the 2,100-seat Concert Hall became of prime importance, so the firm moved the instrument to newly added space behind the upstage wall of a new concert platform that replaces the old concert shell and, in effect, converts a multipurpose proscenium theater into more of a pure concert hall. The new concert platform becomes an apse to the rest of the hall—its upstage wall holds new, nonspeaking façade pipes for the relocated organ—and hews closely to the Walker and Weeks aesthetic for the auditorium, with wood paneling and bas-relief ornament. The floral ceiling pattern used in the auditorium and concert platform was taken from the lace of Mrs. Severance's wedding dress.

The firm's renovation process emphasized the public role of the building. On the

Site plan

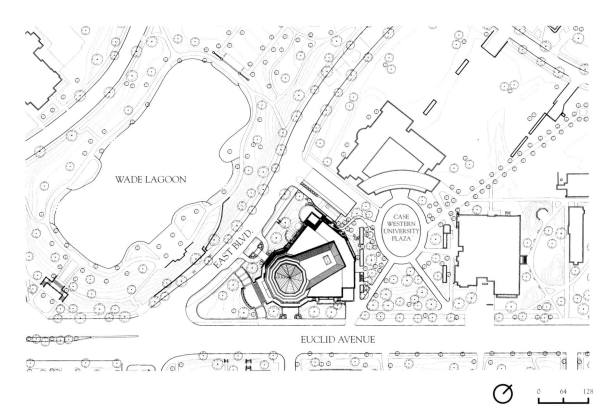

WADE LAGOON

EAST BLVD.

CASE WESTERN UNIVERSITY PLAZA

EUCLID AVENUE

0   64   128

Opposite: Detail of New Plaza Façade. Addition to Severance Hall creates a new "front" for the building's neighbors. The firm designed a new "Severance Order"—stylized Ionic—for pilaster capitals and specified details on this elevation that complement rather than compete with Walker and Weeks' original building.

Far left: Dining Terrace. New public terrace on the East Boulevard side provides outdoor eating area and engages building with its surroundings.

Left: New Terrace Detail. Stone details on new limestone addition (in background) take cues from original (in foreground).

Below: Northeast Façade. New addition commands the green of Case Western Reserve University Plaza.

exterior that goal involved creating a new "plaza façade" at the rear oriented toward a recently completed plaza at the heart of the Case Western Reserve University campus. It is difficult to distinguish the new addition by the Schwarz firm from the original building—the new materials are identical to the old and will weather to match—though it contains modest variations on Walker and Weeks' neoclassical theme in a new "Severance Order" of pilasters, which stylizes the Ionic order by supplanting standard volutes at the capital with musical motifs.

When an underground garage diverted patrons toward the hall's rear, much of the building's public character was lost along with the grand entry procession Walker and Weeks designed to take people from the hall's civic façade to its rich, dramatic interior. The firm largely reclaimed this sequence by formalizing a makeshift corridor to the hall from the garage. This corridor became a series of articulated circulation spaces lining either side of the Reinberger Chamber Music Hall on the ground floor. These axial public spines adjoin spaces for the entrance lobby, gift shop, coat checks, function rooms, musician

lounges, and a new restaurant.

The firm completely restored Severance Hall's significant eclectic interiors, which mix Art Deco with neoclassicism and Egyptian Revival, and provided new backstage, administrative, and storage areas. Technically, the hall gains new life with modern lighting, communication, and sound systems that allow the orchestra to broadcast and record its performances for global audiences. The public's affection for the orchestra and for Severance Hall made both institutions great, and this rehabilitation of the hall ensures that the public will continue to benefit from their combined legacy.

Box-level plan

1. Boardroom
2. Donor suite anteroom
3. Donor suite
4. Box-level seating
5. Organ chambers

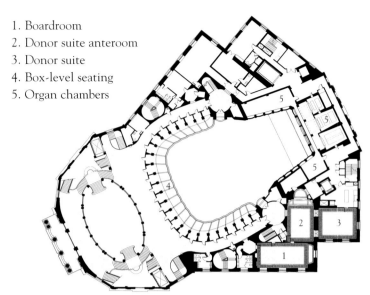

Orchestra-level plan

1. Reception room
2. Reception lounge
3. Grand foyer
4. Orchestra-level seating
5. Green room

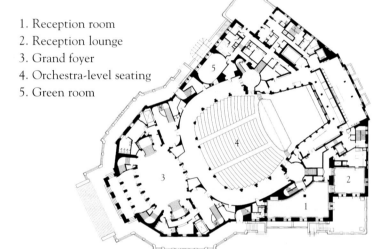

Ground-level plan

1. Limestone entrance (from garage)
2. Patrons' lobby
3. Ong side gallery
4. Lerner side gallery
5. Smith lower lobby
6. Box office entrance vestibule
7. Restaurant
8. Musician lounges and lockers
9. Reinberger Chamber
   Music Hall

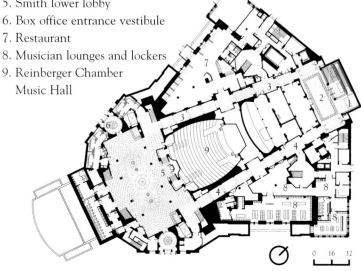

0   16   32

Box-level plan (before)

Orchestra level-plan (before)

Ground-level plan (before)

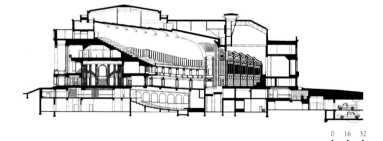

Section

0   16   32

Opposite, top left: *Patrons' Lobby Detail.* Patrons' lobby, the entrance lobby from garage, suggests transition from outdoors with limestone walls, plantings, and faux trellis around skylights.

Opposite, top right: *Patron's Lobby Detail.* New sequence of lobby spaces leading from underground garage is finished in same or similar materials as grand foyer and other front-of-house spaces.

Opposite, bottom left: New Lerner Side Gallery. Newly articulated circulation spaces modulate length of public corridors that take patrons from patron's lobby to front on ground level and up to Grand foyer. Material palette coincides with that of front of house.

Opposite, bottom right: New Coat Check Detail. Materials of support spaces allude to the palette of the concert platform's new grille. Coat check features decorative grille, marble surrounds, new light fixtures based on original patterns, and redeployed original signage.

Left: Detail of Portable Bar in Smith Lobby. Portable bar units provide flexibility. Half bar (shown) fits easily into a corner. Two halves can join to form an "island" bar.

Below: New Ground Level Smith Lobby. New Smith Lobby beneath existing grand foyer offers additional gathering space for patrons and access to restrooms. Terrazzo floor, Deco light fixtures, and marble wainscoting derive from materials used for front-of-house spaces.

Opposite: Restored Grand Foyer. Original details of patterned terrazzo floor, Deco light fixtures, and marble columns influence material choices for new spaces.

Opposite, top left: Renovated Boardroom Detail. Boardroom restored to its original grandeur.

Opposite, left: Detail of Apse in Ginn Donor Suite. New patron lounge, shown set for dining, incorporates decorative wood paneling, coffered ceilings, and custom light fixtures.

Opposite, bottom: New Restaurant. Dining space with elegant period details overlooks lagoon beyond doors.

Top left: Concert Hall Before Restoration. View before renovation shows orchestra shell inserted in 1958.

Top right: Restored Proscenium and New Concert Platform. Redesigned concert platform reinstates Skinner pipe organ. Materials and finishes respond to original Walker and Weeks specifications for Concert Hall interior.

Bottom: Detail of Concert Platform Side Wall. Acoustical success of redesigned concert platform relies on curved wall surfaces, stepping down of side walls, and sloping ceiling of orchestra shell. Open grillework admits sound from Skinner pipe organ to hall volume.

Following pages: Renovated Concert Platform. Concert Hall's painted finishes were restored and aluminum filigree of ceiling paint pattern was cleaned and partially re-leafed. Proscenium arch returns to original Walker and Weeks design to integrate concert platform as extension of Concert Hall.

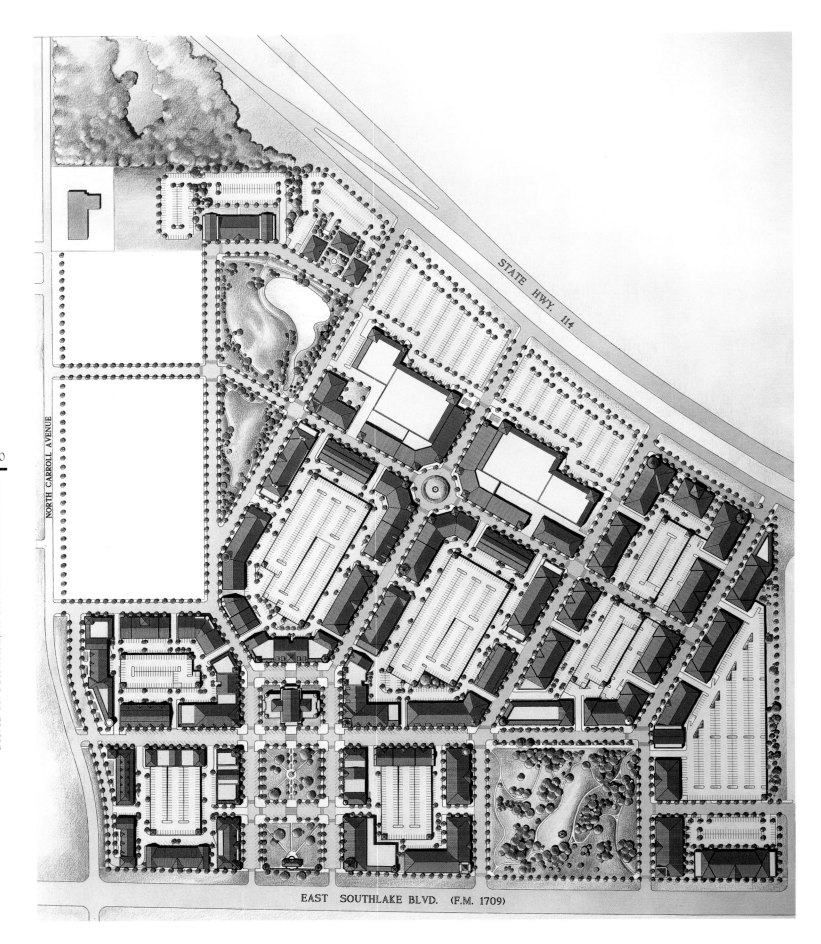

DAVID M. SCHWARZ/ARCHITECTURAL SERVICES

NORTH CARROLL AVENUE

STATE HWY. 114

0   100   200   500

SOUTHLAKE TOWN SQUARE

Southlake, Texas
1997–Ongoing

In the generic suburban landscape north of the Dallas–Fort Worth metroplex, Southlake Town Square presents a heartening anomaly. Whereas strip malls and outsized retail superstores randomly line the surrounding major roads in exclusive service to the automobile, Town Square's 40 acres of retail, restaurant, and office development unfold along a tight, walkable street grid like that of traditional American towns such as Charleston, Savannah, and Annapolis (each of which informed this design). The plan for this new town center fosters cross-socialization, owing to its mix of commercial uses, and its buildings achieve a

vibrant density that pedestrians find appealing. Yet the scheme addresses automobile use realistically: It accommodates motorists with ample parking, but it subordinates the automobile's importance to the prerogatives of people on foot. The design of Southlake Town Square distills the firm's two decades of experience in neighborhood preservation and translates its mandates into neighborhood creation.

The plan, which covers 135 acres to be developed over 10 years, rationalizes a complicated site: The major east-west roads at the perimeter are not parallel, rendering an irregular site geometry, and the topography varies. Town Square's interior street grid maintains orthogonal regularity by intersecting two grids, one oriented to Route 1709 on the south, the other oriented to State

Highway 114 on the north. Around these grids, three parks provide open green space for the town; the largest of them, at six acres, holds a stately collection of live oaks.

The built portions of Town Square depart from standard local zoning regulations to reinterpret the forms of an archetypal American Main Street, which places buildings and sidewalks in mutual engagement. The plan stipulates no setbacks, allowing buildings to rise directly from sidewalks and frequently project into them, with articulated bays, corner towers, and display windows that help define a hierarchy of building entrances and call attention to important block corners.

Collectively, the buildings' façades differentiate so as to appear to have arrived in various styles during different periods, forming storefront

ensembles that reinterpret the vernacular of American—especially Texan—towns. Beneath these variations, however, the firm planned the buildings in 25-foot modules to order their development—typical storefronts run between 25 feet and 100 feet in length, in multiples of 25 feet, which corresponds to their structural grids and to the width of the smallest storefronts. Exteriors of brick, stone, cast stone, and synthetic stucco come alive with details of corbelled and polychrome brickwork, oriel windows, display windows, corner turrets, canopies, awnings, and signage. Most of the buildings have a second-story sill line in common; where roofs appear, they are covered in copper or synthetic slate.

The arrangement of various building masses gives Town Square its character and imparts

Opposite: Site plan.

Above: Town Square. A one-acre civic square forms the heart of Southlake Town Center.

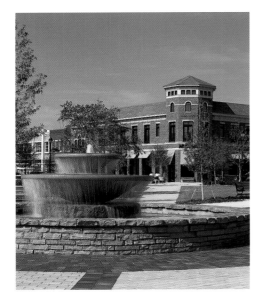

Above: Fountain at Town Square. Fountains enliven Town Square's outdoor spaces and provide a cooling respite from the hot Texas sun.

Right: Detail of site plan showing initial commercial buildings, Town Square, bandshell, and Southlake Town Hall.

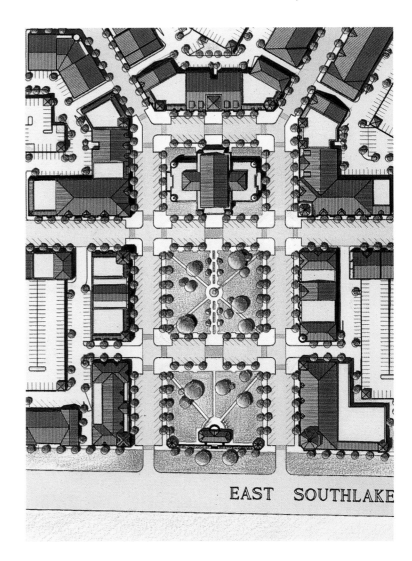

EAST SOUTHLAKE

Typical first-floor plan

1. Retail
2. Office lobby
3. Pedestrian thoroughfare

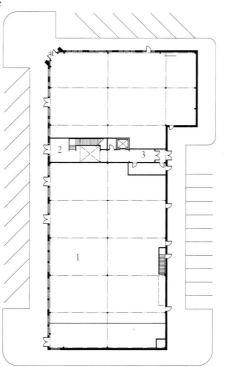

Typical second-floor plan

1. Office
2. Office lobby
3. Restroom

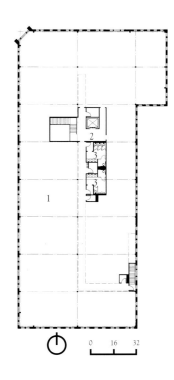

0   16   32

Above: Corner of Grand Avenue and East Southlake Boulevard. Corner massing provides visual anchor at main entrance to Town Square. Polychrome and detail add visual interest.

Below: View to North Along State Street. Building façades vary intentionally in width, detail, materials, and stylistic expression.

the specificity of place, but the need to provide parking commanded nearly as much investigation. The plan sets block dimensions small enough for pedestrian amenity yet large enough to build future parking garages at the centers of blocks. Blocks fall into two classes, larger blocks and smaller blocks that subdivide the larger blocks into pedestrian-scale lengths and provide access to central surface parking. When development on any given block exceeds that which surface parking can accommodate, the plan calls for construction of garages at the block's center, woven into the massing composition at a height of about 32 feet to match that of typical buildings. The supply of on-street parking creates a natural buffer between pedestrians and moving traffic.

Civic life took hold readily in Southlake Town Square, not least with the completion of Southlake Town Hall (pages 200–205), which brings local residents to the neighborhood for routine business. The range of shops, restaurants, services, and offices, totaling 300,000 square feet, draws crowds throughout the day and evening, as do public performances and festivals. Trees, period lamps, benches, pools, and fountains in the streetscape encourage people to linger outdoors. After decades of increasingly careless development in fast-growing areas like the metroplex, it comes as an epiphany to see the public spontaneously embrace a traditionally planned town center. Town Square, alongside its other advantages, provides a convincing critique of the modern development all around it, and it makes sense in ways that bear repeating.

Opposite: Corner of Grand Avenue and Main Street. Articulations of building masses emphasize important corners.

Right: Block Elevation. Rendering shows continuous second floor sill height culminating in turret marking the corner.

Below: View to South Along State Street. An underlying structural grid preordains façade breaks. Landscaping, awnings, and signage enhance intimate pedestrian scale.

Left: Corner of Main Street and Grand Avenue. A simple clip, rather than a tower, marks this corner.

Below: Town Square Park. Commercial façades along State Street form backdrop to the civic square.

Right: Corner of Grand Avenue and Civic Place. Hexagonal corner tower derives from 30-degree bend in Grand Avenue.

Below: Grand Avenue Façade. The tight brick skin and crisp punched openings of this building show the range of styles employed at Town Square. The semi-engaged "drum" tower identifies the entrance to the ground-floor shop and marks the bend in Grand Avenue.

Left: State Street Façade. Façade rhythms vary to disguise rigid second-floor office grid and serve as a stylistic aid, as in this design derived from the Texas Deco period.

Below: Town Square Park. The civic square spreads before Southlake Town Hall (*at right*), serving as the focus and anchor of downtown development.

Right: Façade Bay Marking Pedestrian Passageway. Several buildings have an open-air passage to parking in rear and provide access to office lobby.

CITY OF SOUTHLAKE & TARRANT COUNTY

SOUTHLAKE TOWN HALL

Southlake, Texas
1999

In its contemporary way, Southlake Town Hall marks a return to traditional expression in civic architecture, a recovery of conscience—lost after World War II—about the symbolic imperative of public buildings. Town Hall presides over the main square of Southlake Town Square (pages 190–199) in the spirit of Texas' many great courthouse squares: Its authority is unmistakable, yet it projects a compelling openness we equate with democracy. It occupies the most prominent position in Town Square, clarifying the priorities of an enlightened society.

Town Hall's pink granite stair rises honorifically from the center of the town green on the south to an ochre-colored cast-stone portico of stylized Ionic columns. Behind this two-story portico lies the double-height volume of the main lobby, from which two large lateral wings extend. The articulation of these wings relieves the mass of the four-story, 80,000-square-foot building in a series of several folds with corbelled corners and a fourth-floor attic set back behind a parapet. The skin glows with the sienna color of the velour brick, which contrasts intensely with highlights of ochre cast-stone balustrades, arched surrounds, pediments, and spandrels around the single and paired windows. The Texas lone star recurs as a motif throughout the exterior ornament as it does on the interior.

Beyond an entrance vestibule and small foyer, the main lobby opens up in a manner that is quintessentially Texan. Stylized Doric columns lift from the terrazzo floor to support a perimeter balcony of upper galleries with white stick railings, backed by walls with wood wainscot paneling, coffers, and trim. On the east, the lobby adjoins the council chambers, a double-height space lined with four pilasters behind the council dais, stained-wood wainscot panels and trim. The room seats more than 100 people with overflow balcony space. The balance of the main floor holds a courtroom and court chambers, the justice of the peace, and offices for the town and for Tarrant County. The ground floor holds the city's first public library. Once inside the main lobby, visitors can look squarely through the sequence of entrance spaces onto the town green and instantly recognize that this new building grandly carries forward the history of its genre.

Site plan

Opposite: Portico at Town Square. Town Hall's south elevation faces Town Square with a portico raised on a formal set of steps to signify the building's civic importance. In the fall of 2001, the flags flew at half-staff in memory of the September 11 attacks on the United States.

0   60   120

Main-floor plan

1. Main lobby
2. Council chambers
3. Courtroom
4. Court administration
5. Justice of the Peace
6. Tarrant County Constable
7. Public safety office
8. Human resources
9. Executive conference room
10. City secretary
11. Utility billing

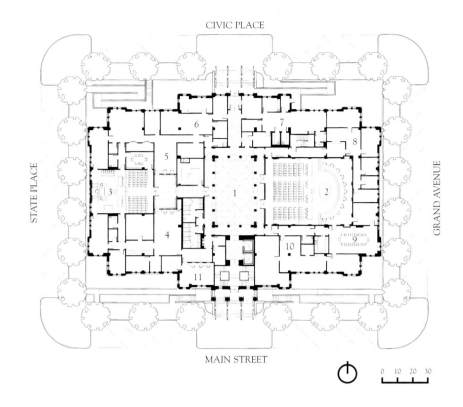

Below: Main Street Elevation. Exterior design of Town Hall refers to the character, scale, and materials of traditional town halls and county courthouses throughout the state of Texas.

Right: Detail at Main Street. Town Hall is richly detailed and broken down in scale by corbelled and custom-shaped brickwork, granite, and two textures and colors of cast stone.

Below right: View from Portico. Town Hall's main entrance and portico rise upon a set of steps overlooking Main Street and Town Square.

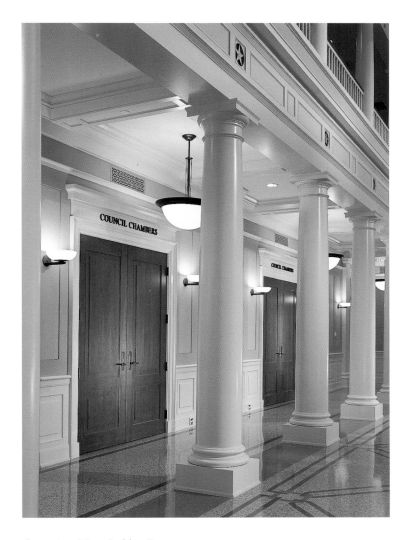

Opposite: Main Lobby. Four-story Town Hall is planned around a central double-height lobby articulated with a perimeter colonnade and ambulatory at both the second and third floors.

Above: Detail of Main Lobby. Main floor and ambulatory have details of traditional wood wainscot paneling and trim, fabric-wrapped acoustical panels, terrazzo flooring, and incandescent light fixtures.

Above right: Council Chambers. Double-height Council Chambers seats more than 100 people, with upper-level balcony seating for overflow. The room's details include traditional stained-cherry wainscot paneling and trim.

Right: Courtroom. This courtroom serves as both the Municipal Court of the City of Southlake and as the local Sub-Courthouse for Tarrant County. Natural light enters the courtroom on either side of the judge's bench.

GUESTHOUSE

Montana

2000

On a site overlooking the Rocky Mountains in Montana, the firm combined the Arts and Crafts aesthetic of Greene and Greene with native rustic influences in the design of this self-sufficient guest house, which sits several hundred yards from the main house on the property.

The walk from the main house leads along a path across a small footbridge constructed of lodgepole pine logs detailed in the same manner as the wood members of the house. The slow rise of a terraced stair leads around a battered stone wall to a spacious terrace that acts as an outdoor living room in front of the house's west elevation. Where the terrace meets the guest house, stone piers support a log trellis that provides a transition from outdoors to the interior.

The 1,800-square-foot guest house reads as a trio of smaller bungalowlike pavilions with pitched, gabled roofs covered in cedar shake shingles, where rough-hewn log rafters emerge and partly protrude from beneath the wide eaves. The massing of the west façade steps back toward the north and east to modulate the guest house's apparent scale. The

largest of these pavilions, at the center of the composition, holds an open combination of living room, dining room, and kitchen. To its south runs a bar-shaped wing for the master bedroom and bath; to its north lies a slightly smaller wing with two guest rooms, one furnished with bunk beds.

Generous windows and clerestories create warmly daylit interiors and frame clear views of the mountains to the west. Mahogany panels and built-in casework line the perimeter of the great-room and bedrooms. The great-room focuses on a fireplace inglenook. Hand-glazed Arts and Crafts tile surrounds the traditional Rumford-style fireplace, and matching benches are built into the nook on either side of it beneath a large mantel and several niches for displaying pottery and other artwork. The mahogany panels continue to

the kitchen area—which subdivides from the main great-room space across a granite-topped island—and rise up to meet integral color plaster walls that join the wood ceiling, which, with its large, exposed wood beams, expresses the house's outer form.

The same roof form defines the ceiling of the master bedroom, which is simply appointed to preserve a dramatic view of the mountains. In the guest bedroom in the north wing, a shallow paneled niche recedes from the high wood-wainscoted walls to frame a pair of beds and nightstands designed for the room in the Arts and Crafts style. The expression of the interior balances richness and restraint, earthiness and refinement, to translate the rugged ecology of the mountain wilderness into the domestic realm.

Floor plan

1. Great room, including kitchen
2. Master bedroom
3. Guest bedroom
4. Bunk room

Opposite: Rear Terrace and Bridge Across Ravine. The guest house sits adjacent to a small ravine on a ridge where the land drops off and the site yields to scrub oak. A small bridge crosses the ravine as part of a path from the main house to the guest house. Rear terrace is faced in stone and serves as outdoor living room overlooking valley.

Above: Rear Terrace and Trellis. Massing of guest house breaks into a series of small pavilions resembling bungalows, with pitched, gabled roofs. Stone piers support log trellis, which shades great-room windows and makes transition between outdoor terrace and interior.

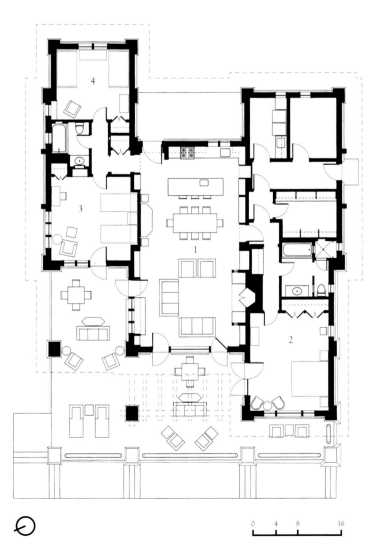

Left: Great Room. The great room, a single, voluminous space, separates the guest wing from the master suite. The walls are built of a high Arts and Crafts–style mahogany paneling with integral color plaster above. The wood ceiling holds a series of large beams and is lit by custom chandeliers of hand-forged black iron with alabaster panels.

Bottom left: Fireplace Inglenook. The living room portion of the great room focuses upon a fireplace inglenook. Hand-glazed Arts and Crafts tile from Matowi Tile Works surrounds a traditional Rumford-style fireplace. A matching pair of small benches allows one to sit close to the fire and enjoy its warmth. The paneling that surrounds the entire room extends to form a large mantel and series of niches to display pottery and small artworks.

Bottom right: Kitchen. The kitchen occupies the east end of the great room. High mahogany paneling surrounds room to form traditional kitchen cabinets and conceal refrigerator. Large granite-topped central island separates working area of kitchen from dining area and great room.

Right: Guest Bedroom. Shallow paneled niche in guest bedroom interrupts high wood-wainscot to hold pair of custom-designed beds and nightstands. Walnut furniture combines American Arts and Crafts and American Rustic details. Beds have accents of hand-molded decorative tile.

Bottom: Master Bedroom. The Master bedroom remains simply detailed to emphasize spectacular view of mountains to west. Pitch of ceiling expresses roof slope and increases volume of room. Pair of wrought-iron-and-alabaster chandeliers hangs from ridge beam. Bed and nightstands are reproductions of Arts and Crafts pieces.

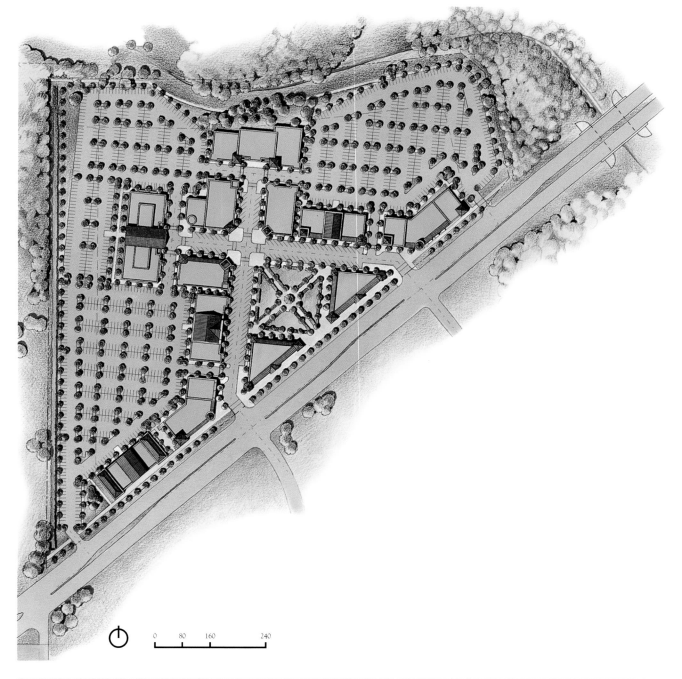

0   80   160   240

PARKER SQUARE

Flower Mound, Texas
1997–Ongoing

The site of Parker Square, which lies 10 miles north of Dallas–Fort Worth International Airport, might have been subsumed by the sprawl of tract housing, strip shopping centers, and scattered office buildings that feed off of Cross Timbers Road, the major traffic artery through suburban Flower Mound, Texas. The site was originally zoned to hold three stand-alone office buildings on a loop road. The firm's client, who had bought the site from another developer, planned to build retail structures with offices above them and leave room for pad-site restaurants and a bank. In 1996, however, the firm persuaded the client and city to modify the zoning guidelines to create a compact neighborhood center mixing retail and commercial uses with parking at the rear. Its framework of traditional planning and eclectic regional architecture provide identity and focus to a suburban area that previously had little physical sense of community.

The 24-acre site is slated to hold 350,000-square feet of shops, offices, service-oriented businesses, and a health club. Two perpendicular streets— one north-south, the other east-west—enter the neighborhood from Cross Timbers Road, carving out a central town green that is between them, landscaped with lawns, trees, and a large pavilion at its heart. The storefront buildings lining both streets along the park rise to two stories (as zoning rules dictate) with articulated corner elements— collectively summarizing the Texan and American traditions of town development, which occurs in various styles and economies. Façades differ in color and detail—those with modest ornament of cast-stone bands and arched window surrounds give way to more richly textured masonry, deeply punched windows, brick pilasters with corbelled capitals, and cornice moldings.

The plan for the neighborhood provides angled streetside parking, but conceals most parking spaces behind the rows of buildings, segregating it from both the town green and from Cross Timbers Road. Parker Square subverts the car-dependent paradigm governing suburban development and suggests a compromise: It is possible to plan around the automobile without sacrificing the pedestrian character of our cities and suburbs.

Opposite, top: Site Plan. Parker Square's compact street plan segregates parking behind retail/ office buildings.

Opposite bottom: View to West from Square. Shops and restaurants with second-floor office space overlook the square. In background at center, a building's main entry forms terminus of one of the neighborhood's main streets.

Right: Façade Detail. Corbelled brickwork underscores second-floor window rhythm and creates level of detail scaled to pedestrians. Structural-steel lintel and columns supporting masonry veneer become integral components of storefront design.

Elevation detail

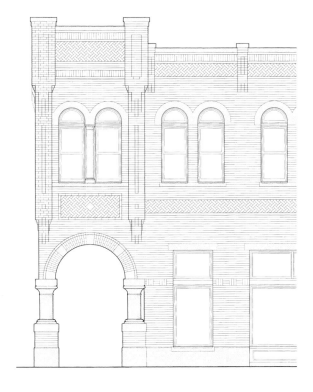

Opposite, top: Square with Building 900 in Background. An octagonal pavilion marks center of square. The first of the development's 12 buildings, Building 900, has a strongly centered, symmetrical façade overlooking the square.

Opposite, bottom: View from Parker Square Pavilion. The domed corner tower terminates the diagonal vista from the pavilion located in the middle of the neighborhood square.

Right: South Façade of Building 400. This 40-foot-wide façade at main intersection uses corbelled brickwork to articulate the parapet and reinforce the window rhythm. Larger corbels and a step-up in the parapet draw the eye toward the corner, where at street level, two generous arched openings harbor a recessed entrance.

Opposite, top: Building 600. The corner of Building 600 was deemed the neighborhood's most important façade, owing to its marking of the main intersection and siting opposite the entrance to the square. The cupola-topped dome with clock caps a rounded inset portico at the corner retail entrance and creates an appropriately civic-minded commercial icon for the neighborhood.

Opposite, bottom: Twenty-Foot-Wide Façades of Building 400 ("The Three Sisters"). The three façades in the foreground are identical in width and window rhythm but differentiated by brick color, window geometry, and masonry detailing.

Right: Detail of Building 600. Decorative cast-stone blocks and polychrome brickwork break down the deep spandrel panels necessitated by building's structural system. Corbelled and polychrome brickwork compose stylized capitals.

Below: Façades of Buildings 300, 400, and 500. Zoning regulations restrict buildings to maximum height of two stories, therefore, parapets vary in height and detailing to create complex silhouettes.

CHATEAU ST. JEAN

Sonoma Valley, California
2001

A surge of popularity proved paradoxical for Chateau St. Jean, a relatively small winery in Kenwood, California, that belongs to the Beringer portfolio of high-end vintners. Favorable reviews of several Beringer wines in the 1990s brought droves of people to three of its properties in northern California's wine country, but the volume of visitor traf-

fic threatened to overwhelm the grounds of each. In 1998, Beringer hired the firm to devise master plans for its historic winery in St. Helena, the small estate winery of Stag's Leap north of Napa, and Chateau St. Jean, where the firm also designed a 5,000-square-foot hospitality building and reorganized the site around a series of walled display gardens. The redesign and new construction at Chateau St. Jean improves visitors' ability to move about the site, while maintaining the formal focus on the chateau and the vineyards on the hillside.

The new master plan for Chateau St. Jean reduces the visitor parking area of the site, but not the number of parking spaces. The firm planned a series of cloistered courtyards within garden walls and rationalized the formerly con-

fusing entrance sequence so that it culminates in an intimate entrance court marked by a trellis.

Another trellis, atop a high wall, separates the gardens from the parking area. Visitors enter through either of two matching pavilions that lie on axis with the main circulation path and lead to small courtyards next to the new hospitality building. At the center of the main garden stands a fountain; a statue of St. Jean appears on the edge of one of the central parterres. The decomposed-granite paths of the main garden have low hedges and clay pots lining them. The new garden design relies on large existing trees for shade over benches and lawn areas.

Within this renovated plan for the grounds, the firm was able to add the hospitality

building with minimal impact on the presence of the chateau and the landscape—its shorter façade faces onto the far end of the main garden. The hospitality building's materials—pale stucco walls, red clay roof tiles, and cast-stone trim—respond to those of extant buildings on the site.

On the interior of the hospitality building, the main space measures 3,000 square feet and holds a bar for wine tastings, a charcuterie, and retail space beneath fir trusswork supporting the roof. Dominating the room's long wall is a mahogany bar with a zinc top. The back bar houses wine refrigerators, lighted display cabinets, and a charcuterie. During wine tastings, French doors with fan lights above them open into terraces and gardens, allowing a smooth flow between the interior and the verdant outdoors.

Elevation

Site plan

Opposite: Garden with Hospitality Building. New hospitality building occupies far end of new walled garden, which is organized around a central fountain and a statue of St. Jean. Separate parterres defined by paths connect parking lot with smaller entrance courtyards. The garden, designed with Olin Partnership Landscape Architects, incorporates existing large trees, a demonstration vineyard, and seasonal plantings.

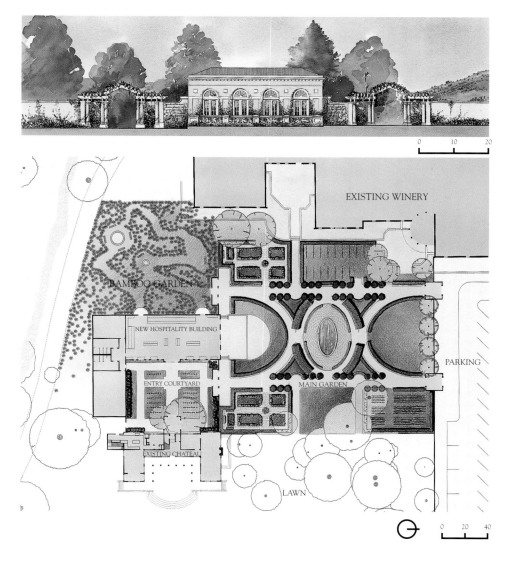

Left: Main Path to Entry Garden. At far end of walled display garden, visitors enter new hospitality building from small entrance courtyard that separates it from existing chateau. Redwood trellis marks openings in garden wall. Paths are decomposed granite.

Below: Entry Courtyard with Main Entrance to Hospitality Building. Small entrance courtyard opens before hospitality building. Between courtyard and main garden stands a high wall beneath a redwood trellis. Steel-and-glass canopy protects entrance to building.

Right: Main Trellis with Oil-Jar Fountain. Cast-stone columns support redwood trellis to provide shaded space for repose. Oil-jar fountain provides sound of running water. Potted plants add color just inside garden walls.

Below: Hospitality Building and Wine-Tasting Terrace. Wine-tasting terrace extends interior space of hospitality building to the outdoors. French doors allow visitors to move easily between these two spaces, and garden furniture offers a place to relax.

Left: Hospitality Building and Main Garden at Dusk. Hospitality building glows through French doors during evening hours, when visitors may schedule tours and tastings. Lighting design imparts atmosphere of small country estate.

Below: Hospitality Building Entrance. Lighting design allows outdoor spaces to accommodate evening events without detracting from night sky.

Right: Interior with Tasting Bar. Mahogany bar with zinc top lines long wall of main room in hospitality building. Wood trusses span full width of room and support ceiling of milled fir trees that formerly occupied site.

Below right: Hospitality Room with Charcuterie. Tasting room holds charcuterie at far end with custom-designed display cases that match tasting bar.

YALE ENVIRONMENTAL SCIENCE CENTER

New Haven, Connecticut
2001

The built history of Yale University posed formidable questions for the firm as it began designing a new 100,000-square-foot Environmental Science Center in an area of the campus known as Science Hill, between the venerated green space of Sachem's Wood and the Peabody Museum of Natural History. Science Hill, which covers 37 acres, lacks consistency in the siting and design of its buildings, most of which are modernist structures developed during the mid-20th century. Foremost, the firm believed that the center's design should continue the tradition of Collegiate Gothic architecture that predominates within the university's old central campus several blocks to the south down historic Hillhouse Avenue. The building visually ties Science Hill back to the old campus and rectifies modernist planning by reviving the spirit of earlier site studies by John Russell Pope and James Gamble Rogers. It also satisfies numerous programmatic concerns with great coherence and beauty, yielding a building that upholds the finest aspects of Yale's architectural legacy in an eminently progressive spirit.

The massing, siting, and exterior language of the three-story center combine to form a gateway into Science Hill. The building stretches south to north to define the eastern edge of Sachem's Wood, a sloping green with a collection of mature trees, much as the Collegiate Gothic Osborn Memorial Laboratory completes the wood's western edge. It joins the Collegiate Gothic–style Peabody Museum to the east with the Kline Geology Laboratories to the north, creating a natural-sciences compound with an active flow of faculty and students.

The firm studied numerous examples of the Collegiate Gothic style, including those at Oxford and Cambridge as well as later American iterations at Washington University, the University of Chicago, and Princeton, to discern the particular language of Yale's buildings. The firm drew off of, among other features, Yale's complex fenestration patterns, wherein two-panel windows may range above and below three-panel windows. The logic of the massing capitalizes on asymmetries common in the Collegiate Gothic. The gabled bays that bracket the west façade are larger and their fenestration differs from that of the central bays (which have clasping buttresses consistent with the Yale variety of the style) to maintain the façade's balance, given the relatively heavy presence of the octagonal tower to the southwest. This tower unites the building's two fronts—one facing west to Sachem Wood

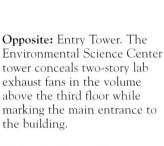

Opposite: Entry Tower. The Environmental Science Center tower conceals two-story lab exhaust fans in the volume above the third floor while marking the main entrance to the building.

Right: Southwest Corner at Sachem Street. The Environmental Science Center, as paired with the exemplary Neo-Gothic Osborn Memorial Laboratory, terminates the northern end of Hillhouse Avenue and creates an appropriate gateway from its tree-lined avenue of old mansions to the complex of larger institutional buildings that comprise Science Hill.

Site plan

1. Environmental Science Center
2. Peabody Museum of Natural History
3. Sachem's Wood
4. Science Hill campus
5. Osborn Memorial Laboratory
6. Kline Geology Laboratories
7. Kline Biology Tower
8. Main campus core

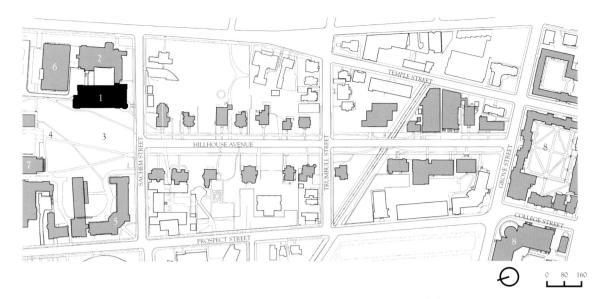

224

Third-floor plan

1. Entomology collections
2. Botany Herbarium collections
3. Paleobotany collections
4. Entomology collections management
5. Botany Herbarium collections management
6. Paleobotany collections management
7. Research laboratory
8. Researcher office

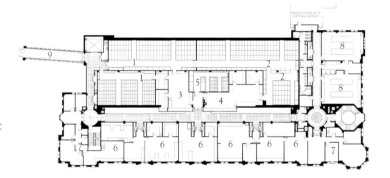

Second-floor plan

1. Invertebrate Zoology collections
2. Invertebrate Paleontology collections
3. Invertebrate Zoology collections management
4. Invertebrate Paleontology collections management
5. IP/IZ Library
6. Research work room
7. Researcher office
8. Teaching laboratory
9. Bridge to Kline Geology Laboratory Building

First-floor plan

1. Vertebrate Zoology collections
2. Vertebrate Zoology collections management
3. Vertebrate Zoology library
4. Research laboratory
5. Researcher office
6. Classroom
7. Center for Earth Observation

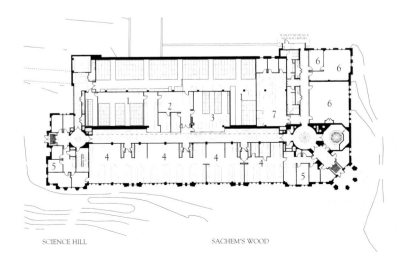

and the other facing south to Sachem Street—and opens three arches to the deeply cloistered main entrance between corner buttresses. The long west façade facing the wood has more windows than the south façade and they occur in a regular rhythm to express the likeness of the laboratories that align on each floor of the interior. By contrast, the south façade's fenestration has irregular cadences denoting the varied offices and classrooms it holds. It includes an oriel window framed, as they all are, in a deep-red cast stone, which foils the softly sparkling skin of red and ironspot brick laid in a Flemish bond.

Five University departments occupy the building—Forestry and Environmental Sciences; Geology and Geophysics; Anthropology; Ecology and Evolutionary Biology; and the Peabody Museum of Natural History—and the interiors arrange around cogently detailed public spaces. The main entrance leads to a vestibule with wainscoting of Texas Cordova shell-stone panels encased in Cordova Cream limestone surrounds, within which fossilized remains hint at the building's scientific purpose. This wainscot continues into a domed rotunda lobby, the floor of which displays one of the building's several circular terrazzo patterns drawn from nature—some have leaves laid in a sunburst pattern, another depicts quartz crystals. To the south of this lobby rises an open octagonal stair tower, in which railings of aircraft cable line the stairs circling upward at the perimeter in a flood of natural light.

Spaces for research and teaching form an L-shape along the public (western and southern) sides of the center—the considerable balance of each of the three floors contains compact storage for the Peabody collections. From the rotunda lobby, a brief corridor extends east toward classrooms and offices, and a much longer circulation spine runs the north-south length of the plan, between the outer modules of flexibly stationed research labs on the west and the Peabody offices and collections seen behind an interior curtain-wall façade on the east—effectively uniting the building's two distinct constituencies. All of these circulation spaces carry a rich wainscot of blue Mexican tile. The long circulation axes of each level stack up beside the interior curtain wall within a spatially arresting light well atrium where the floors are left a bare black concrete slab. Full-height walls on either side of the curtain wall reflect light off of large Venetian plaster panels that cast a rich, yellow hue into the atrium.

Both the public face and the interior of the Environmental Science Center radiate warmth uncommon in research facilities. The disposition of labs and learning spaces furnish a contemporary framework emphasizing the social component of scientific investigation. The totality of the design advances the idea that collective knowledge inheres greater value than isolated discovery, and that answers to questions of science, as those of architecture, prove most relevant when they rejoin something larger than themselves.

Above: Lab Gable on Sachem's Wood Façade. The scale of ESC's architectural elements relate to those on buildings in Yale's Collegiate Gothic core, though some details relate to 20th-century buildings on Science Hill. Flemish bond brick echoes that of neighboring buildings—the ironspot brick resembles that on Kline Geology Laboratories and field brick resembles that on Peabody Museum.

Right: Sachem's Wood Façade. The ESC defines the eastern edge of Sachem's Wood to create a campus park from what was a loosely bounded 3-acre open space at the base of Science Hill.

West-east section

1. Collections
2. Research laboratories
3. Laboratory support
4. Circulation
5. Mechanical

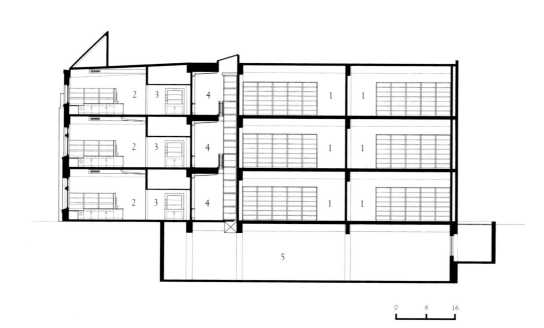

0   8   16

Above left: South Stair Bay on Sachem Street. This gable on the south façade identifies the bay for the south stair, hinting at the multistory space inside. This bay terminates the main north-south circulation spine and admits natural light down its length.

Above right: Northern Gabled Bay of Sachem's Wood Façade. The largest gabled bay on the ESC marks the north end of the western façade while allowing the mass of the building to pass through and terminate in a slightly smaller bay facing north.

Opposite: Sachem's Wood Façade. The ESC's details quote elements specific to Yale's version of Collegiate Gothic (clasping buttresses, arches, gabled bays, entrance porticos) in consistent proportions and combine them with modern inflections across a façade that responds to the site at the edge of Sachem's Wood. Syncopation of window patterns is unique to the ESC and its site, but similar to rhythms found throughout the Yale campus buildings of James Gamble Rogers and Charles Haight.

Left: South Stair from Third-Floor Landing. The skeleton of the dinosaur *Deinonychus antirrhopus*, discovered by a Yale professor and Peabody curator, hangs in the ESC's main stairwell. The southern, or classroom, end of the building contains terrazzo floors throughout. Floors of main stair and rotundas hold terrazzo medallions of floral and geological motifs.

Below: South Stair. Railings throughout the building were detailed for maximum transparency to allow openness, light, and clear perception of each room's volume. The refinement of details, proportions of rooms, and height of bay windows continues tradition of ceremonial staircases within Yale's academic buildings.

Opposite: Entrance Lobby from Landing of South Stair. Interior arrangements pay careful consideration to the quality of light as one proceeds through the building. Rotundas mark the cross-axes at each end of the building beneath the brightest levels of artificial light. Transitions between the rotundas and naturally lit central light well are purposefully darker. All public corridors terminate at naturally lit space.

Left: Light Well, View from First Floor. This three-story space serves as the building's central commons, transforming what would have been three long, dark, uninterrupted corridors into a warm, spacious room. From the skylight above the third story, light floods the building interior through the 5-foot-wide light well, which runs the length of the 150-foot-long room, interrupted only by the glass-enclosed research space for collections managers.

Above left: Collections Management, View from Light Well. Managers and staff of each collection work in the glass box along the Venetian plaster wall, receiving secondary natural light from skylight above, which keeps harmful direct sun away from artifacts. Bridge across light well provides only access to collections, allowing collections managers to act as gatekeepers to artifacts.

Above right: Second-Floor Light Well, View Toward South Stair. All public corridors of the ESC terminate in naturally lit spaces. More than nine million specimens of the Peabody Museum collections are stored in areas behind yellow Venetian plaster wall.

Right: Research Laboratory Interior. Research labs align along west wall of ESC, facing Sachem's Wood. Ceilings remain open to give rooms greater height and to allow for addition of future piping and ductwork, and are darkly painted to allow all the varied items to blend together. Reagent shelving was deliberately painted white to add brightness and openness to the room. Labs modify easily for hard science or for use as work rooms for less-intensive research.

AMERICAN AIRLINES CENTER

Dallas, Texas

2001

Opposite: North Entry Arch at Sunset. The arena's grand arches spring more than six stories high to welcome the city to the interior. The arches open into the building's entrance lobbies and offer patrons unique views of Dallas.

Below: East Façade Along Houston Street. The large gesture of the vaulted roof responds to its purpose of enclosing a 20,000-seat arena. Massing of building breaks down into smaller segments along the façade to activate the sidewalk and create a pedestrian-friendly experience.

Historians will find a broad, authoritative shift of building iconography in the firm's design of the American Airlines Center, a 20,000-seat multipurpose arena that opened in July 2001 as the home of the Dallas Mavericks basketball team and Dallas Stars hockey team. The transformative power of the building recalls that of Daniel Burnham's 1908 Union Station in Washington, D.C. Burnham found no classical precedent for a railroad station of its magnitude and thus reinterpreted the Roman forms of the triumphal arch and the public bath to render the station as a grand civic gateway. Likewise, in the design of the American Airlines Center, the firm avoided most recent examples of arena architecture, which tend to be hostile to human factors, and sought inspiration in other large-scale building typologies—among them railroad stations—that can accommodate the multitudes yet modulate in scale to relate to pedestrians. The rail-station analogy has potency, too, because part of the site, a planned urban development known as Victory, formerly served as a rail yard. And though the American Airlines Center does not resemble a rail station per se (notwithstanding inevitable comparisons to Eliel Saarinen's marvelous station in Helsinki), from a distance it achieves a similar sense of monumentality in the urban landscape while responding to the needs of the individual at close range.

Having emerged as the developer's choice in a 1998 invitational competition involving four other internationally known firms, the firm's first major task was to help formulate an urban plan for the 60-acre Victory site in which to situate the arena. As with the master plan for the Ballpark in Arlington (pages 92–103), the firm imagined the site's future as one of dense, pedestrian-oriented development that would also receive a high volume of automobile traffic. A new street grid connects the Victory site to the street grid of Dallas's downtown, West End, and arts district. At the firm's urging, the city's transportation department reconfigured plans for a nine-lane highway into two more pedestrian-friendly one-way streets where people can park during non-rush hours.

The firm positioned the arena's rectangular footprint at the heart of Victory to frame views of downtown through the south façade and to complete

Left: South Entrance Façade from Victory Plaza at Night. The arena's south façade becomes the backdrop for Victory Plaza, a two-acre civic gathering space that complements the arena with public art. Three star-shaped fountains, created by artist Athena Tacha, activate and cool the space. The fountains turn off to allow large outdoor events, such as concerts or farmers' markets.

Site plan

1. West office/retail
2. Victory plaza
3. East office/retail

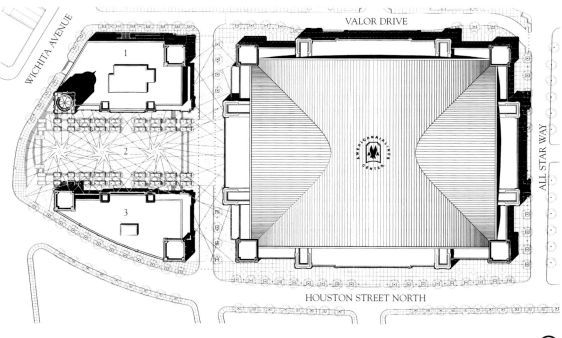

Below: Façade Detail of Entrance Arch, Logo, and Vaulted Roof. Exterior details create visual interest. Highly variegated brick enlivens flat surfaces. Stepped brick-and-limestone patterns provide interesting play of light and shadow across façade. Pattern of vaulted roof was designed by artist Vicki Scuri as part of public art program.

Bottom: Northeast Corner Tower. Arena's four corners articulate as tower elements to anchor vaulted roof and define street edge clearly. Corner towers contain street-level specialty retail stores and concessions, bars, and conference space on upper levels.

Bottom right: North Façade Looking Across Houston Street. The façade reflects the arena's program: arched opening provides views to five circulation concourses; vertical stair towers anchor arch; arched roof covers bowl; and corner towers anchor roof and define street edge.

the view corridor of Payne Street on center with the east façade. Near the west façade, the city plans to locate a mass-transit station. The north façade becomes the first view one sees on the approach from the Stemmons Freeway. The south façade also faces a two-acre public plaza of fountains and star-patterned paving, around which the firm has also designed future retail and office structures on either side to bracket downtown's view of the arena and mediate between the arena's larger scale and that of the future surrounding neighborhood.

Scale, however, is not a concern that the arena's design relegates to collateral structures—its careful calibration is evident in the arena's deliberately binary massing and in the rigorous control the firm keeps over the general plan. The slope of the 150,000-square-foot

double-barrel-vaulted roof identifies the larger scale of the building—it is a coup of imagery but of economics as well, optimizing the number of structural-steel members it requires for support. The roof's barrel vaults overarch the full width of all four facades. Each façade, in turn, begets secondary readings of a smaller scale with sculptural graduations of height from the corners to the center, and with syllabic expressions of interior functions wrought in the walls' depth (such as the extruded emergency-exit stair towers flanking the central bays, which, along with the corner towers, relieve the expanse of these walls and emphasize the building's vertical aspect). An abundance of rhythmic window perforations focus upon large, arched central openings, and the envelope shows artful exterior detailing:

striated surfaces of ironspot brick, Indiana limestone bands, and a base of Swedish mahogany granite. The building incorporates $2.4 million worth of public artworks.

The exterior design evolved in tandem with the arrangement of four perimeter lobbies surrounding the arena's seating bowl. These large, sometimes quadruple-height lobbies, located on the main concourse level inside entrances on the north, south, east, and west and connected by smaller lobbies between them, act as straightforward orientation devices for visitors. Each lobby looks into or over the adjoining lobby and out to the city through an exterior glass wall; the views enable people to mark their location far more easily than the common "racetrack" circulation found in many modern arenas. Where large and small

1. Lower seating bowl
2. Lower suites
3. Club seating bowl
4. Upper suites
5. Upper seating bowl
6. Main lobby
7. Lower suite mezzanine
8. Club-level concourse
9. Upper suite mezzanine
10. Upper gallery concourse
11. Club restaurant
12. Service level
13. Spotlight platforms/
    acoustical bass trap
14. Press box
15. Basketball practice court
16. Mechanical rooms
17. Club-level balconies

Preceding pages: North Façade Approach Along Victory Drive. Arena becomes the front door of Dallas as motorists approach the city from the north. Double-barrel-vaulted roof offers memorable image as seen from highway but recedes behind primary street elevations at closer range.

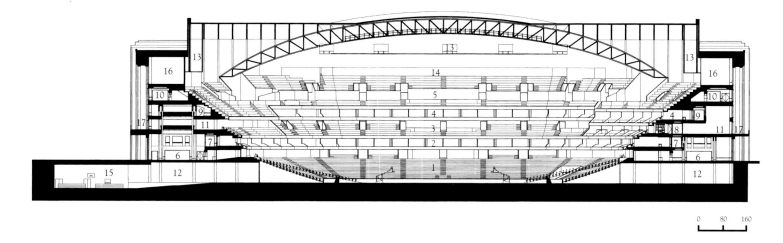

0   80   160

Main concourse plan

1. South lobby
2. West lobby
3. North lobby
4. East lobby
5. Rotunda
6. Corner lobby
7. Concessions/merchandise
8. Team store
9. AA city ticket office
10. Stars/Mavericks Club bar
11. Retail
12. Box office
13. Premium seatholder entrance
14. Lower seating bowl
    (basketball configuration)

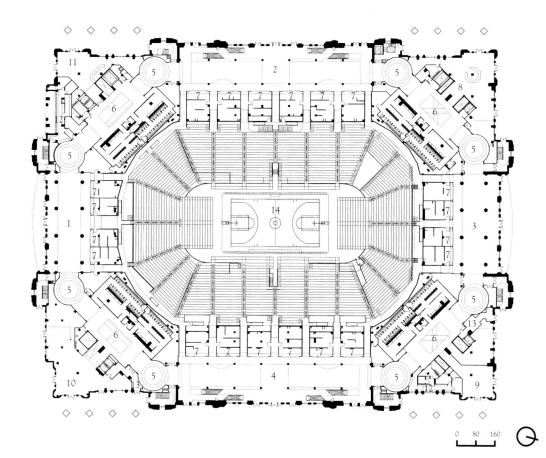

0   80   160

Below: Detail of Terrazzo Floor Pattern. Arena's terrazzo floors provide durable walking surface and integrate artwork into design. Intricate patterns reinforce building's structural grid and recall stepping motif of exterior detailing.

Bottom: Detail of Rotunda. Eight five-story-high rotundas create turning points between large and small lobbies, adding visual dynamism among multiple lobby levels.

Bottom right: South Lobby Looking West at Club Restaurant. Fifty-foot-high columns define south lobby and vertically link first four levels of arena, allowing patrons to interact among levels of grand public room. Space contains scale models of sponsor American Airlines' aircraft fleet throughout its history.

lobbies join, the firm incorporated circular turning points—five-story-high rotundas—that finesse the transition between distinct regions of the building. The hierarchy of these visually interwoven lobby spaces also becomes clear in their spatial manipulation—the large lobbies expand to hold vertical circulation systems, the concession stands, and access to the seating-bowl vomitories, whereas the smaller lobbies compress by comparison, as they house restrooms and secondary functions for the arena.

The material palette of these public circulation spaces dignifies visitors in ways uncommon for large arenas, which typically leave all structural surfaces exposed or simply painted for the sake of wear. The lobbies of the

American Airlines Center assume a civic mood. Smooth, clean wall finishes serve as backdrops to ranks of octagonal columns marching along the lobbies' edges with ribbed capitals highlighted in aluminum. Terrazzo floors throughout the main and upper concourses set a vibrant staging for railings, light fixtures, signage, and advertising icons of brushed aluminum, stainless steel, and glass. Ornament, as ever in the firm's work, is of a piece with the architecture.

The concourse areas are replete with patron amenities: a total of 37 concession stands, two bars, several retail stores selling team merchandise, and two ticketing locations. More than 10,000 square feet of flexible meeting and banquet space is available throughout the various levels.

The dramatically deep seating bowl, the geometry of which inverts that of the spectacular

curving roof trusses above it, converts readily from an 18,000-seat configuration for hockey to 19,200 seats for basketball and can hold an additional 800 seats for concert events. This is an absorbing space for spectators, separated into three main tiers—lower, club, and upper seating—divided by two levels of suites at the sides. At the bowl's north end, the club-level seats discontinue to hold suites, and that level's south end houses a restaurant and bar with views directly into the bowl. It is a testament to the painstaking programming, planning, and stacking of the American Airlines Center that patrons can find themselves nearly anywhere within its interior and still have excellent views of the events on the floor.

Left: East Lobby at Main Concourse. The building's wayfinding signage integrates into building design and becomes part of decoration. Large arched openings act as intuitive wayfinding devices, providing views to city, and flood each of four lobbies with daylight.

Below left: West Lobby Looking South from Lower Suite Level. Arena's interior circulation moves patrons through a series of well-defined rooms. West Lobby vertically links main concourse with lower suite and club levels and contains escalators to upper concourse. Terrazzo floors, railings, column capitals, and stepped ceilings combine in understated yet sophisticated level of detail.

Below right: Main Concourse of East Lobby. Side aisles off main lobby space contain ancillary program areas, including concession queuing on main concourse, which is tucked between vomitories to the bowl-circulation mezzanine for access to lower suites; and club-level circulation concourse. Curved balcony provides space for portable concessions at club level.

Opposite: Lobby Stair. Rich detailing recalls tradition of civic structures throughout history. The steel, terrazzo, and aluminum stair boldly expresses its functional and aesthetic purpose. Orthogonal lines of maple and glass bars on club level contrast with curvilinear lines of terrazzo below.

Left: Marché Dining and View of Upper Suite Mezzanine. The club level's less-formal restaurant, the Marché Dining Room, features a cocktail bar and two food bars that prepare meals à la carte. Suspended upper suite lounge overlooks this space, which can serve as a large meeting room or reception hall.

Below left: Hockey Rink View from Club Restaurant. Club restaurant provides direct views to event floor in addition to seating around the south lobby and outdoor seating overlooking Victory Plaza. The restaurant's finishes include bamboo floors, mahogany woodwork, and verde grissone marble counters.

Right: Typical Suite View of Hockey Rink. The typical suite contains 16 seats with clear sight lines to the event floor. Additional club chair seating and stools at kitchen bar allow for intimate conversations. Dedicated suite kitchens provide food and beverage service to each of the arena's 140 suites on four levels.

Below: Lower Suite and Suite Seating Ring. Located directly above lower seating bowl, the arena's 64 lower suites provide individuals and corporate patrons the opportunity to attend events in private suites finished in a timeless palette of French limestone, black granite, leather, and natural maple casework, and outfitted with the latest technological innovations.

East-west section

1. Lower seating bowl
2. Lower suites
3. Club seating bowl
4. Upper suites
5. Upper seating bowl
6. Main lobby
7. Lower suite mezzanine
8. Club-level mezzanine
9. Upper suite mezzanine
10. Upper gallery concourse
11. Club restaurant
12. Service level

13. Spotlight platforms/acoustical bass trap
14. Press box
15. Loading dock

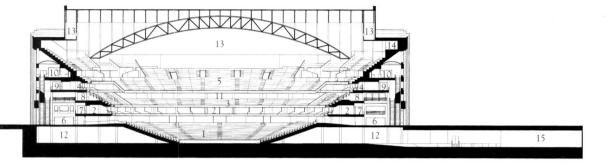

0   80   160

DAVID M. SCHWARZ/ARCHITECTURAL SERVICES

Right: Detail of Interior Roof Truss. The 3½-acre roof is supported by a series of 11-foot-deep curved trusses that slope down to seating bowl's four corners. Four corner trusses rest on floor of upper concourse. Roof's weight transfers to four concrete columns while series of steel rods embedded in upper concourse floor counters corner columns together and ties roof's outward thrust.

Far right: Seating Bowl and Hockey Rink from Lower Suite Level Looking South. Supported at its four corners, the vaulted roof is expressed by its curving trusswork enclosing the arena.

Seen here in hockey configuration, the seating bowl design maintains optimal sight lines for a variety of events. Upper suite ring stops short on south end where upper deck pulls down and forward.

Below: Seating Bowl and Hockey Rink. The Dallas Stars play beneath the largest eight-sided scoreboard in the world. In addition to lower and upper decks, the arena has three levels of suites behind the "shoot-twice" end of the rink. A continuous, 30-inch-high band of electronic advertising circles seating bowl below club level.

BIBLIOGRAPHY

02/06/02	*Yale Alumni Magazine* "Designed for Science"	Yale Environmental Science Center
01	*Developing Sports, Convention and* *Performing Arts Centers*—Urban Land Institute David C. Petersen—Third Edition	Bass Performance Hall Ballpark in Arlington
11/12/01	*Texas Architect* "First Step to Victory"	American Airlines Center
11/06/01	*Washington Post, (Arts/Backstage)* "Dramatic Development"	Mount Vernon Walk
11/01	*Landscape Architecture* "Simply Stellar—Subtle details add life to a new public plaza in Dallas"	American Airlines Center
11/01	*Architectural Record* American Preservation: Revering the Past "Cleveland's premier symphony space is returned to grace"	Severance Hall
10/30/01	*Fort Worth Star-Telegram* "A serious musical workout brings out best in recital hall"	Maddox-Muse Center
10/01	*United Airlines Hemispheres* magazine "Three Perfect Days in Dallas"	West Village
10/01	*International Design* magazine "Sound Ensemble"	Bass Performance Hall
09/02/01	*The New York Times* "In Fort Worth"	Bass Performance Hall
09/01	*D* magazine "Style in the City"	American Airlines Center West Village
08/01	*D* magazine "City of David; 'The ballpark and the arena came first. David Schwarz is rethinking Dallas'"	David Schwarz
07/29/01	*Dallas Morning News* "Center Stage—'A classy joint'; 'Like a hotel', 'Wow'"	American Airlines Center
06/11/01	*Miami Herald* "Fort Worth's stunning Arts Center is a glorious ode to city's past"	Bass Performance Hall
06/19/01	*Moscow Pravda* "And the gilded trumpets of the Fort Worth angels"	Bass Performance Hall
06/01	*New Urban News* "New urbanists critique projects"	Southlake Town Square
05/25/01	*Cleveland Plain Dealer* "New auditorium, new way of ranking at Cliburn contest"	Bass Performance Hall
05/24/01	*Cleveland Plain Dealer* "Cleveland Orchestra finds Texas hall fitting"	Bass Performance Hall Severance Hall
05/23/01	*Fort Worth Star-Telegram* "Out-of-town orchestra is out of sight at Bass"	Bass Performance Hall
04/01	*Architecture* "Fitting into the Historic Fabric"	Maddox Muse Center

3–4/01	*Texas Journey* magazine "Everything Old is New Again; 'Fort Worth's cultural revolution continues'"	Bass Performance Hall
3–4/01	*Preservation* magazine "Pipe cleaner"	Severance Hall
02/22/01	*Design Architecture News* "Giddy-up! National Cowgirl Museum and Hall of Fame by David M. Schwarz"	National Cowgirl Museum and Hall of Fame
1–2/01	*New Urban News* "Public Policy"	Frisco Town Square
01/01	*Masonry Construction* "Top Projects of 2000"	Maddox Muse Center
10/00	*AIA/DC News* "2000 Chapter Awards: The Jury is In! Winners Announced"	Severance Hall
08/00	*Contract* "Exquisite Euphony"	Severance Hall
04/12/00	*Yale Daily News* "A Major League university: Yale's baseball connection"	Ballpark in Arlington
04/00	*WHERE Dallas* "The Architect's Hall of Fame"	David Schwarz
02/00	*Properties Magazine, Inc.* "Bravo!!! The Glorious Restoration of Severance Hall"	Severance Hall
01/22/00	*Washington Post* "Urban Squeeze on the Avenue"	The Saratoga
01/19/00	*Financial Times* "Warming up the Szell shell"	Severance Hall
01/15/00	*The Toronto Star* "Breaking the sound barriers"	Severance Hall
01/10/00	*Cleveland Plain Dealer* "Severance superb on small scale, too"	Severance Hall
01/10/00	*The New York Times* "No, They didn't take away that Hall's lovely sound"	Severance Hall
01/09/00	*Cleveland Plain Dealer* "Perfect Harmony-'Old, new seamlessly joined at Severance Hall'"	Severance Hall
01/09/00	*Cleveland Plain Dealer* "The music, the magic are back at Severance— 'Design stunning; acoustics hold promise'" "Bravos for Severance"	Severance Hall
01/02/00	*Dallas Morning News* "Lone Stars for the 21st Century"	David Schwarz
01/02/00	*Cleveland Plain Dealer* "The Restoration of Severance Hall"—entire section	Severance Hall
01/02/00	*Washington Post* "In Cleveland, a Concert Hall's Comeback"	Severance Hall

BIBLIOGRAPHY

01/02/00	*The New York Times* "Cleveland Orchestra is getting it's home back"	Severance Hall
01/00	*Architectural Record* "After a restoration, music is heard again at Cleveland's much-lauded Severance Hall"	Severance Hall
01/00	*Masonry Construction* "Best Institutional/Public Building— 'Nancy Lee and Perry R. Bass Performance Hall'"	Bass Performance Hall
09/7/99	*Dallas Morning News* "Bass Hall's angelic angles provide geometry lessons—'18,000 FW students to study building in math program'"	Bass Performance Hall
08/30/99	*Cincinnati Enquirer* "Ballpark in Arlington looks better from the outfield"	Ballpark in Arlington
08/29/99	*Cincinnati Enquirer* "A Search for the perfect ballpark" "A ballpark comparison"	Ballpark in Arlington
Summer/Fall 99	*Tarrant Points West* "Buildings as Art"	Bass Performance Hall Maddox-Muse Center Angeluna
Summer 99	*Contemporary STONEdesign* magazine	DMS Interview
06/12/99	*Fort Worth Star-Telegram* DETAILSdetails "Bolt to the Tool Box Bash"	Habitat for Humanity
05/6/99	*Texas Architect* "Saving Downtown"	American Airlines Center
05/99	*UrbanLand* magazine "Downtowns Get a Sporting Chance"	American Airlines Center
05/99	*Yale Alumni* magazine "Architects Meet on Remaking Yale"	Environmental Science Center
05/99	*Architectural Record* "The Art and Science of Sound" "Architects & Acousticians must listen to one another to integrate good design and good acoustics in performing arts centers"	Bass Performance Hall
03/14/99	*Fort Worth Star-Telegram* "Southlake's expectations for its first downtown include unifying a growing city" "Architect puts an emphasis on comfort and convenience"	Southlake Town Square David Schwarz
3–4/99	*Architectural Specifier* magazine "A Bit of Dallas"	Fort Worth Sundance Square
03/99	*Travel & Leisure* magazine WHERE TO GO NEXT—"Top Ten Opera Houses"	Bass Performance Hall
02/19/99	*Wall Street Journal* "Raising the Roof"	Bass Performance Hall
02/99	*Stone World* magazine Limestone in Architecture "Working within the limits"	Bass Performance Hall
Winter 99	*blueprints*—National Building Museum "David Schwarz's Sense of Place"	David Schwarz

12/98–01/99	*Travel/Holiday* magazine "A new breed of Texas longhorn? Yes! In Fort Worth"	Bass Performance Hall
09/98	*Building Design & Construction* "Community Theater—A new $45 million multi-use performance hall gives voice to the songs of Fort Worth"	Bass Performance Hall
09/98	*Urban Land* magazine "Trumpeting the Arts in Fort Worth" (by DMS) "A New Downtown Arena and More" "Dallas/Fort Worth Real Estate Markets— Hotter than Hot"	Bass Performance Hall American Airlines Center Southlake Town Square
08–09/98	*TCI—Theatre Crafts International* "Texas Tradition—The new Bass Performance Hall brings a European-style opera house to Ft. Worth"	Bass Performance Hall
08/9/98	*Dallas Morning News* High Profile: David Schwarz "Building for people and not other architects"	David Schwarz
08/98	*Building Design & Construction* magazine "Design Chosen for New Dallas Arena: Washington, D.C.-based architect leads design team on $230 million project"	American Airlines Center
08/98	*D* magazine "The Architectural Counter-Revolution: Why David Schwarz is the right architect to build the new arena"	American Airlines Center
07–08/98	*SYMPHONY* magazine "Heralding a New Era: Fort Worth unveils a new concert hall of landmark proportions"	Bass Performance Hall
07/18/98	*CLASSICAL music* magazine "Culture Comes to Cowtown—'Angels in Cowtown'—Fort Worth's new hall"	Bass Performance Hall
07/98	*Washingtonian* magazine "Forgey has good architecture eye"	David Schwarz
07/98	*Architectural Record* "Texas Summer Heating Up As Big Names Battle for Commissions"	American Airlines Center
06/98	*Architecture* "Lone star rising"	Bass Performance Hall
06/26/98	*PERFORMANCE* magazine "Bass Hall—Fort Worth's Newest Prize Catch"	Bass Performance Hall
06/20/98	*The Toronto Star—Arts* "The house that Texan pride built— Bass is one of the great concert halls of the century"	Bass Performance Hall
06/3/98	*Miami Herald* "Fort Worth arts center may hold lesson for Miami"	Bass Performance Hall
05/28/98	*Austin American Statesman* "Music becomes a sensual experience at Fort Worth's new Bass Performance Hall"	Bass Performance Hall
05/23/98	*Washington Post* "Ushering in the 19th century"	Bass Performance Hall
05/22/98	*Wall Street Journal* "Cowtown goes classical"	Bass Performance Hall

BIBLIOGRAPHY

05/12/98	*The New York Times* "What's new in concert halls? A taste for the Old"	Bass Performance Hall
05/12/98	*Realty Times* "The New Urban Village: The Town Square Makes a Comeback in Texas"	Southlake Town Square Sundance Square
05/9/98	*Dallas Morning News* "All-star extravaganza opens FW's Bass Hall"	Bass Performance Hall
05/6/98	*Texas Architect* "Of Note: Grand Openings"	Bass Performance Hall
05/3/98	*Fort Worth Star-Telegram* "Place of Grandeur" "Hall of Contrasts"	Bass Performance Hall
05/98	*D* magazine "Concept and Design— 'Four top architecture designers describe what an arena can do'"	American Airlines Center
05/98	*Civil Engineering* magazine "State of the Arts—Engineers dealt with the challenges of a multilevel horseshoe seating pattern and critical acoustical considerations to provide a world-class performing arts center in Fort Worth, Tex."	Bass Performance Hall
04/25/98	*Houston Chronicle* "A Hall for the Centuries"	Bass Performance Hall
04/14/98	*Seattle Post-Intelligencer* "If concert halls of Dallas, Fort Worth are an example, Benaroya should be a success"	Bass Performance Hall
03/8/98	*Cleveland Plain Dealer* "Severance expansion plan excellent"	Severance Hall
05/7/97	*Fort Worth Star-Telegram* "The last great hall this century"	Bass Performance Hall
03/23/97	*Cleveland Plain Dealer* "Severance Renovator's home runs"	Severance Hall
01/26/97	*Washington Post* "Disney: A Good Sport"	Disney's Wide World of Sports
06/9/96	*Fort Worth Star-Telegram* "The Renaissance of a city's heart—Flurry of projects is putting the hustle and bustle back into a downtown that was in decline five years ago"	Fort Worth Projects
07/8/95	*Historic Preservation* "Urbane Renewal"	Fort Worth Projects
11/95	*Brick in Architecture* "The Ballpark in Arlington"	Ballpark in Arlington
07/16/95	*Austin Statesman* "Architect Lives & Learns"	Ballpark in Arlington
07/95	*Interiors* "Schwarz Designs Hall for the Performing Arts"	Bass Performance Hall
06/95	*Landscape Architecture* "Texas Leaguer"	Ballpark in Arlington
06/95	*Architectural Record* "Paris on the Seine—Or Fort Worth on the Trinity"	Bass Performance Hall

06/94	*Architecture* "D.C. Architect Designs Civic Projects in Texas"	Bass Performance Hall Ballpark in Arlington
06/94	*Progressive Architecture* "A Performance Hall for Ft. Worth"	Bass Performance Hall
05/94	*Civil Engineering* magazine "A League of Their Own"	Ballpark in Arlington
05/2/94	Real Estate Finance "Baseball Cities Pitching for Development"	Ballpark in Arlington
04/14/94	*The New York Times* "At Home in the City, Baseball's Newest Parks Succeed"	Ballpark in Arlington
04/12/94	*USA Today* "Home Run at the Ballpark"	Ballpark in Arlington
04/12/94	*Washington Post* "The Eyes of Texas Are Upon the Opening of the Ballpark"	Ballpark in Arlington
04/12/94	*Fort Worth Star-Telegram* "Architect's Idea Unites Old, New" "It's Official: Rangers Make Move to Ballpark"	Ballpark in Arlington
04/11/94	*Washington Post* "Texas' New Ballpark: Put This One in the Win Column"	Ballpark in Arlington
04/11/94	*Dallas Morning News* "Opening Day Reveals Grand New Ballpark"	Ballpark in Arlington
04/10/94	*Houston Chronicle* "Rangers finally hit big time on patch of prairie"	Ballpark in Arlington
04/10/94	*Washington Post* "Deep in the Heart of Texas" "Schwarz, Changing the Landscape"	Sundance West Bass Performance Hall Cook Children's Medical Center 1718 Connecticut Avenue
04/10/94	*Fort Worth Star-Telegram* "Unveiling a Potential for Greatness"	Bass Performance Hall
04/07/94	Dallas Morning News "Grand Designs"	Bass Performance Hall
04/07/94	*Fort Worth Star-Telegram* "Performance Hall to Mix Old, New" "A Performing Arts Hall for Fort Worth" "David Schwarz: Performance Hall"	Bass Performance Hall
04/04/94	*Wall Street Journal* "New Ballparks Give Fans an Old-Time Feeling"	Ballpark in Arlington
04/03/94	*Tulsa World* "A Whole New Ballgame" "Rangers's New Park a 'Showpiece': It May be the 'Best Ballpark in the World'"	Ballpark in Arlington
04/02/94	*Dallas Morning News* "First-Pitch Home Run" "Ballpark a hit in sparkling debut"	Ballpark in Arlington
04/02/94	*Fort Worth Star-Telegram* "Play Ball!" "They came, they saw...they loved it!" "The Ballpark's a hometown hit" "Major-league day for North Texas"	Ballpark in Arlington

BIBLIOGRAPHY

04/01/94	*The New York Times* "Rangers Make Their Home Thoroughly Modern Texas"	Ballpark in Arlington
04/01/94	*Fort Worth Star-Telegram* "It's Awesome"	Ballpark in Arlington
04/01/94	*Dallas Morning News* "The Ballpark is everything it was built up to be"	Ballpark in Arlington
04/94	*Dimensional Stone* "Rock Solid 'Veteran' Boosts Rookie Stadium into Big Leagues"	Ballpark in Arlington
03/31/94	*Fort Worth Star-Telegram* Souvenir Section "The Ballpark in Arlington" "Details, Details"	Ballpark in Arlington
03/31/94	*USA Today* "New Ballpark—Doubleheader"	Ballpark in Arlington
03/94	*Texas Architect* "Cowtown Downtown"	Sundance West Sanger Lofts
03/94	*The Business Press* "Playball!"	Ballpark in Arlington
10/31/93	*Dallas Morning News* "Dream It, He Will Come"	Ballpark in Arlington Bass Performance Hall Sundance West Cook Children's Medical Center
10/93	*Aura* of Fort Worth "Downtown Cowtown Pioneers" "Lofty Living in One Desirable Downtown"	Sundance West Sanger Lofts
8/93	*Architectural Record* Lighting Supplement "Scenic Surprise"	Sundance Cinemas
92	*Cite* "Squeeze Play"	Ballpark in Arlington
92	*Design Solutions* "Reel Different Theatre Design"	Sundance Cinemas
92	*AURA* "Winning a Showdown"	Sundance West
92	*The American House* "Design for Living"	The Saratoga
11/92	*DC/AIA News* "Award Recipients"	Sundance Cinemas
07/06/92	*Fort Worth Star-Telegram* "Hospital, Solana Win Building of the Year Awards"	Cook Children's Medical Center
06/14/92	*Dallas Morning News* "Fort Worth: Where Sundance West Begins"	Sundance West
05/92	*Fabricator* magazine "Careful Project Management is Key to Success"	Sundance Cinemas
05/92	*Business Press* "Sundance West"	Sundance West Sundance Cinemas
04/92	*Texas Architect* "Downtown Dreams"	Sundance Cinemas

01/2/92	*Chicago Tribune* "The Big Picture"	Sundance Cinemas
91	*The Best in Lobby Design* "Hotels and Offices"	Cook Children's Medical Center 1133 Connecticut Avenue
91	*The Best in Office Interior Design* "Fairytale Towers"	Cook Children's Medical Center
91	*Child Health Design* "Nurses' Stations—Design Approaches"	Cook Children's Medical Center
91	*LYS/Toli* (Japan), Vol. 9 "Sheer Genius Makes Dreams Real," "Imagination at Play: David Schwarz, Just Like in the Movies"	Design for a Wedding
11/91	*Business Press* "Schwarz Reshaping Tarrant by Design"	Sundance Cinemas
10/91	*Architecture* "Details"	Ballpark in Arlington
10/20/91	*Fort Worth Star-Telegram* "Drawing Power"	Ballpark in Arlington Sundance West Cook Children's Medical Center
09/7/91	*Washington Post* "Washingtonian's Home Run Hit to Texas"	Ballpark in Arlington
09/2/91	*Dallas Times Herald* "New Stadium as Bold as Texas"	Ballpark in Arlington
09/2/91	*Arlington News* "New Ballpark Will Be a Great Place to Call Home"	Ballpark in Arlington
08/30/91	*Dallas Morning News* GRAND SLAM "New ballpark's design is fantastic"	Ballpark in Arlington
08/29/91	*Fort Worth Star-Telegram* "Rangers Announce Architectural Team for New Stadium" "When it's built, they will come"	Ballpark in Arlington
08/29/91	*Fort Worth Star-Telegram* "A Traditional Texas Flavor: Sundance designer is named architect for Rangers ballpark"	Ballpark in Arlington
08/29/91	*Dallas Times Herald* "A Bit of Texas: The Stadium's Facade Would Display Texas Architecture" "Rangers play by stadium rules" "Stadium has flavor of Texas: Park to use elements of Lone Star heritage"	Ballpark in Arlington
06/9/91	*Fort Worth Star-Telegram* "A Renaissance Downtown Goes Uptown: Recapturing a Way of Life from the Past for a More Vibrant Future"	Sundance West
02/1/91	*Business Press* "Sundance AMC Complex to Offer Touch of Ziegfield"	Sundance West
90	*Art for Everyday* by Patricia Conway	Private Residences
10/90	*Give Us Your Best* A Catalog of Washington Architect's Work.	The Saratoga Hollywood Plaza Cook Children's Medical Center Private Residence

10/90	*House and Garden* "Crafting a Style"	Private Residence
10/14/90	*The New York Times: Notebook* "Sundance Units All Pre-leased"	Sundance West
10/6/90	*Washington Post* Well-Built Washington Potpourri: Area architects pick their best."	National Building Museum Show
05/12/90	*National Building Museum Tour* Washington's 12 Best New Office Buildings by James M. Goode	1718 Connecticut Avenue
05/90	*Architectural Record* "Serious Play: For a children's hospital, architect David Schwarz prescribes comfort delight and a big surprise."	Cook Children's Medical Center
04/90	*Interiors Magazine* "Setting a Marriage"	Design for a Wedding
04/90	*Architectural Record* "Design News: A mixture of old and new building on Hollywood Boulevard."	Hollywood Plaza
02/90	*Architectural Record* "The Best and Worst of Washington, D.C."	The Saratoga 1718 Connecticut Avenue 1818 H Street
1–2/90	*Museum & Arts Washington* "Back to the Future: Washington's 1990 Experts Predict"	David Schwarz
11/11/89	*Washington Post* "Connecticut's New Jewel: The Saratoga, at Home on the Grand Avenue"	The Saratoga
09/89	*Home* magazine "Remodeling: Best Remodeling Ideas in America"	Private Residence
05/21/89	*Fort Worth Star-Telegram* "A Medical Wonderland"	Cook Children's Medical Center
04/13/89	*Fort Worth Star-Telegram* "Bass Apartments Get September Start Date"	Sundance West
3–4/89	*New Dominion* "The Kays at Merrywood"	Merrywood
01/14/89	*Washington Post* "Raleighs: A House Judiciously Divided"	1133 Connecticut Avenue
01/89	*Regardie's* "The Power Elite"	David Schwarz
01/89	Custom Builder "McLean, VA"	Merrywood
88	*Best Addresses: A Century of Washington's Distinguished Apartment Houses* by James M. Goode	The Griffin Penn Theater Project
Fall 88	*Regardie's Luxury Homes Washington* "Mixed Metaphor" "Uncommon Places" Interview with David Schwarz: "Mix Master/David Schwarz on His Neo-Eclectic Architecture"	Private Residence Merrywood

7–8/88	*Abitare Magazine* (Italy) "Washington: La Citta-Capitol Hill: The Penn Theater" "La Scoperta del Recupero Alla Ricerca di Una Citta 'Storica'"	Penn Theater Project 1818 N Street 1133 Connecticut Avenue
02/88	*Metropolitan Review* "New Architecture in Washington D.C."	Penn Theater Project 1133 Connecticut Avenue
12/87	*Regardie's* Downtown Design Charrette "Designer Town"	555 11th Street
12/87	*Museum & Arts* magazine	Private Residence
10/87	*Architecture* magazine "Interiors"	Private Apartment Residence
08/87	*Progressive Architecture* "PADC Choice for Landsburgh Site"	Landsburgh Project
04/87	*Architectural Record* "A Contradiction in Terms"	Cook Children's Medical Center
02/21/87	*Washington Post* "Landsburgh's Happy Plethora"	Landsburgh Project
01/11/87	*Washington Post* "City Cafe is the New Jewel in the Town"	City Cafe
12/86	*Washingtonian* "The Good, The Bad, and The Ugly"	Penn Theater Project
11/11/86	National Trust for Historic Preservation Brochure "Revitalizing Urban Business Districts"	1718 Connecticut Avenue
11/86	*Architecture* magazine "Contextualism Continues Strong in the Capital"	Penn Theater Project The Griffin
10/86	*Home* magazine	Private Residence
09/20/86	*Washington Post* "Firm Foundations—A Show of Real World Architectural Drawings"	DMS/ASPC work
07/24/86	*Washington Post* "The seamless, stylish expansion of a cramped Victorian cottage"	Private Residence
06/14/86	*Washington Post* "The Penn is Mightier: David Schwarz's Refreshing Stylistic Diversity"	Penn Theater Project
02/3/86	*Washington Post* "Designer Birthday: Celebrating Schwarz in Art Deco Style"	David Schwarz Birthday Celebration
02/1/86	*Washington Post* "The Architect's Neighborly Approach"	The Griffin
01/86	*Brickwork Design*	1718 Connecticut Avenue
12/85	*Baumeister* (West Germany) "Intarsien Und Mehrfarbigkeit"	1718 Connecticut Avenue
11/26/85	*Newsday* "Some Call It Façadism"	1818 N Street Penn Theater Project
11/85	*Common Bond* "Masonry Designs Receive Top Awards"	1818 N Street

BIBLIOGRAPHY

09/85	*Washingtonian* "First, Chop Down Those Cherry Trees"	1718 Connecticut Avenue Penn Theatre Project 1818 N Street The Griffin
12/15/84	*Washington Post* "Keeping Up a Front: The Fine Façade at 1818 N St."	1818 N Street
11/84	*Architecture* "Finally, Façadism with Finesse"	1818 N Street
07/84	*Architectural Record* "Neo-Eclecticism on the Potomac"	1718 Connecticut Avenue 1818 N Street Penn Theater Project
12/83–01/84	*Regardie's* "Revivalist Fervor"	David Schwarz/ASPC Work
10/1/83	*Washington Post* "When It's Better to Be Blue—A Blue Chip Project"	Penn Theater Project
09/82	*Progressive Architecture* "In Progress"	Penn Theater Project
09/26/81	*Washington Post* "Raising the Roofline: A Classy Addition to Connecticut Avenue"	1718 Connecticut Avenue
09/20/80	*Washington Post* "The Seventh Street Solution"	406 Seventh Street
09/80	*ArtNews* "A Real Renaissance in Downtown Washington"	406 Seventh Street
08/30/80	*Washington Post* "Filling in the Gaps"	1718 Connecticut Avenue
07/27/80	*Washington Star* "The Dawning of a New Soho"	Hanover Arts Project Johnson Avenue
10/9/79	*Washington Star* "Better Buildings"	1718 Connecticut Avenue
10/04/79	*Washington Star* "A Block-Booster, Not Buster"	1718 Connecticut Avenue
09/79	*Washingtonian* magazine	Hanover Arts Project
09/20/79	*Washington Star*	Hanover Arts Project
01/6/79	*Washington Post* "House Fantasies Fulfilled"	DMS Residential Work: 203 Constitution NE 1460 Q St. NW

AWARDS

05/13/02	International Masonry Institute New England Region *2002 Golden Trowel Award for Colleges &* *Outstanding Use of Masonry*	Yale Environmental Science Center
03/12/02	American Council of Engineering Companies Honor Award—Structural Engineering Walter P. Moore *Best Engineering Project in the Nation for 2001*	American Airlines Center
03/5/02	Association of General Contractors of Texas Summit Award *2001 Outstanding Project Over $30m*	American Airlines Center
03/02	*Texas Construction* magazine *Best of 2001 Judges Award*	American Airlines Center
02/27/02	Subcontractors Association of North Texas *2001 Outstanding Project Over $25m* and *Outstanding Project Team*	American Airlines Center
10/19/01	Society of American Registered Architects National Professional Design Awards Program *Design of Honor Award for Recognition of Superior* *Achievement & Professional Design Excellence*	Maddox-Muse Center
10/18/01	National Trust for Historic Preservation National Preservation Award *For the sensitive restoration and expansion of* *Severance Hall, the world-famous home of the* *Cleveland Orchestra*	Severance Hall
05/8/01	United Masonry Contractors Association *Golden Trowel Award for Outstanding* *Craftsmanship in Residential and Other*	Southlake Town Hall
01	United States Institute for Theatre Technology, Inc. (USITT) *Honor Award*	Severance Hall
11/17/00	American Institute of Architects Washington Chapter *Merit Award for Outstanding Achievement* *in Historic Resources*	Severance Hall
10/20/00	Society of American Registered Architects National Design Awards *Award of Excellence—Gold Ribbon*	Severance Hall
09/00	Associated Masonry Contractors of Houston *2000 Golden Trowel Award*	Maddox-Muse Center
09/00	American Institute of Architects Washington Chapter *Award of Merit in Historical Resources*	Severance Hall
Summer/00	The Texas Masonry Council *2000 Golden Trowel Regional Award* *for design elements and craftsmanship*	Maddox-Muse Center
07/00	The Cleveland Restoration Society 2000 Preservation Award *Trustee Honor Award for Presentation Achievement*	Severance Hall

AWARDS

05/25/00	American Institute of Architects Cleveland Chapter *Certificate in Recognition of Exceptional Accomplishment in Areas of Preservation, Restoration, Adaptive Re-use and Maintenance of an Architecturally Significant Building*	Severance Hall
04/29/00	Society of American Registered Architects California Council *Design Award for Excellence*	Southlake Town Square
04/29/00	Society of American Registered Architects California Council *Design Award for Excellence*	Severance Hall
05/99	The Chicago Athenaeum: Museum of Architecture and Design *The American Architecture Awards Program, 1999*	Bass Performance Hall
03/99	Masonry Contractors Association of America (Education/Government Category) Presented to LUCIA for exterior stonework *International Excellence in Masonry*	Bass Performance Hall
03/99	American Institute of Steel Construction Engineering Awards of Excellence *Award of Merit*	Bass Performance Hall
03/4/99	*Texas Architect* magazine American Institute of Architects-Ft. Worth Chapter *Award of Merit*	Disney's Wide World of Sports
01/99	Associated Builders and Contractors *1998 Excellence in Construction* FIRST PLACE	Bass Performance Hall
12/98–01/99	*Holiday/Travel* magazine *Travel Holidays 1999 Insider Awards*	Bass Performance Hall
10/24/97	Society of American Registered Architects *Design Award of Honor*	Sundance East
97	United Masonry Contractors *1997 Golden Trowel Award* . *Outstanding Brick Design*	Sundance East
11/96	Society of American Registered Architects *Award of Merit*	Worthington Hotel Renovation
10/25/96	Society of American Registered Architects *Design Award of Merit*	Worthington Hotel Renovation
02/6/95	American Institute of Architects—Fort Worth Chapter *Certificate of Achievement*	Worthington Hotel Renovation
02/95	Associated Builders and Contractors *First Place—Excellence in Construction awards competition*	Ballpark in Arlington
95	Historic Preservation Council for Tarrant County, Texas *1995 Historic and Cultural Landmarks Commission Award*	Sanger Lofts

11/94	American Institute of Architects Fort Worth Chapter *Recognition*	Ballpark in Arlington
10/21/94	Society of American Registered Architects *Design Award of Merit*	Sundance West
10/94	Society of American Registered Architects *Design Excellence*	Ballpark in Arlington
94	Dallas Business Journal Real Estate Awards *Best Community Impact-Architectural*	Ballpark in Arlington
03/15/93	Associated Builders and Contractors *Excellence in Construction* *Award of Merit*	Sundance Cinemas
93	Associated Builders and Contractors *Outstanding Achievement* *Excellence in Construction*	Sundance Cinemas
93	Illuminating Engineering Society International Illumination Design Awards *Edwin F. Guth Memorial Lighting* *Award of Excellence*	Sundance Cinemas
11/92	American Institute of Architects-D.C. Chapter *Design Excellence*	Sundance Cinemas
11/6/92	Society of American Registered Architects *Design Award of Merit*	Sundance Cinemas
11/6/92	American Institute of Architects-D.C. Chapter *Award for Excellence*	Sundance Cinemas
07/92	Building Owners and Managers Association "In Pursuit of Excellence: *Building of the Year Award*"	Cook Children's Medical Center
91	Society of American Registered Architects (SARA) *Professional Design Awards Program*	1133 Connecticut Avenue Cook Children's Medical Center The Saratoga
91	Texas Rangers Ballpark Design Competition—Contract Award	Ballpark in Arlington
90	Associated General Contractors of America, Ft. Worth Chapter *"Outstanding Building Projects Award"*	Cook Children's Medical Center
90	Landscape Contractors Association *Grand Award—Environmental Landscape Award*	Private Residence
90	American Institute of Architects Architecture for Housing *Design for Living Design Award*	The Saratoga
90	*Interiors* magazine Washington Design Celebration *Competition—Design Award*	Design for a Wedding
89	The Masonry Institute *Special Achievement Design Award*	The Saratoga

AWARDS

88	Landscape Contractors Assoc. Merit Award *Environmental Landscape Award*	Private Residence
88	Landscape Contractors Assoc. DCA Landscape Architects, Inc. *Environmental Landscape Award*	Merrywood
88	The Masonry Institute *Special Achievement Design Award*	1133 Connecticut Avenue
87	The Masonry Institute *Design Award*	Penn Theater Project
86	Mayor's Architectural Design Awards	"Downtown Stages" Theater Study
85	The Masonry Institute *Design Award*	1818 N Street
84	Art Deco Society of Washington *First Annual Preservation Award*	Penn Theater Project
84	The Masonry Institute *Design Award*	1718 Connecticut Avenue

SELECTED LECTURES & EXHIBITIONS

09/01/01   American Institute of Architects (AIA)
Design in Historic Preservation
Old Town Alexandria, Virginia/Washington, D.C.
"Design Issues in Classical Architecture"
Discussion/Slide Presentation of philosophical approach to the renovations at
Severance Hall

03/31/01   Congress on New Urbanism
Charleston, South Carolina
"Southlake Town Square"
Discussion/Slide Presentation

03/29/00   Cleveland Club of Washington
Washington, D.C.
"Restoration of Severance Hall"
Discussion/Slide Presentation: Craig P. Williams, Project Architect, and
Gary Hanson, Executive Associate Director of Severance Hall

03/23/00   University of Notre Dame
Notre Dame, Indiana
"What if Modernism Never Happened"
Lecture/Slide Presentation

01/07/00   Hawken School
Gates Mills, Ohio
"The Expansion and Renovation of Severance Hall as an example of
Architectural and Visual Literacy as it relates to our daily lives"
Upper School & Faculty Lecture/Slide Presentation

10/25/99   Yale University
New Haven, Connecticut
"Environmental Diversity: A Discussion of Style and Context in Architecture"
Lecture/Slide Presentation

10/19/99   Partners for Livable Communities National Conference
"Crossing the Line"
Memphis, Tennessee
Panel Chairman: "Downtown Investment Strategies-Revitalizing the Core"

09/23/99   Greater Dallas Planning Council
Dallas, Texas
"Building Better Cities"
Lecture/Slide Presentation

6/7–8/16/99   The American Architecture Awards—"New Architecture Designed in the United
States" The Chicago Athenaeum/Museum of Architecture and Design, Chicago, IL
(*Exhibit:* Nancy Lee and Perry R. Bass Performance Hall)

04/11/99   Yale Constructs Symposium
Yale University School of Architecture; New Haven, CT
Presentation of Yale University Environmental Science Center

10/23/98   Society of American Registered Architects (SARA) National Convention
Washington, D.C.
"The Roots of the Reds: Washington's Architectural Heritage"
Lecture/Slide Presentation

10/8/98   Urban Land Institute
Dallas, Texas
"The Economics of Architecture"
Lecture/Slide Presentation

SELECTED LECTURES & EXHIBITIONS

09/15/98	National Building Museum (Architects of Downtown Cultural Series) "Building Culture Downtown: New Ways of Revitalizing the American City" *Lecture*
5/1/98–1/3/99	National Building Museum Washington, D.C. "Building Culture Downtown: New Ways of Revitalizing the American City" (*Exhibit:* Nancy Lee and Perry R. Bass Performance Hall)
11/19/97	Texas Tech University Lubbock, Texas College of Architecture "New Life for the American Downtown"
05/1/96	Virgin Cinemas "Theaters and Cinemas"
04/23/96	University of Texas Austin, Texas School of Architecture "Compilation of DMS/AS Projects"
10/17/95	CPA "Relations between the Private and Public Sectors"
10/14/95	American Planning Association "Planning for Entertainment—If You Build, Will They Come?"
09/93	*Traveling Exhibit:* "Field of Dreams: Architecture and Baseball"
05/13/93	Dallas Museum of Art Dallas, Texas "Texas Rangers Ballpark"
04/6/93	Modern Art Museum of Fort Worth Fort Worth, Texas "Toward the Next New Architecture—or When Cathedrals Weren't White"
03/27/93	Trilateral Commission "The Embassies of Kalorama"
03/25/92	The Washington Design Center "Texas Rangers Ballpark and Other Works in Progress"
05/17/91	A.I.A. National Convention "Current Residential Design"
10–11/90	National Building Museum/Washington Chapter A.I.A. "Give Us your Best" (Exhibition and Catalogue)
06/21/90	The Urban Land Institute "The Real Estate Development Process: New Trends in Architecture"
05/04/90	National Building Museum Tour of "Washington's Twelve Best New Office Buildings" with James M. Goode
04/90	The Washington Design Center Winner of The Washington Design Celebration *Competition/Exhibition*

04/17/90	D.C. Preservation League Fifth Annual Gerald D. Hines interest lecture series "Preservation: The Architect's Challenge"
01/25/90	The Smithsonian Institution/National Trust for Historic Preservation "New vs. Old Design: Creating compatible architecture in Washington's historic context"
09/27/88	The Washington Design Center "Washington Today: Architecture & the City"—Seminar.
03/4/88	The Athenaeum "A Decade of Washington Architecture" Exhibition including the Penn Theater Project and 1818 N Street
02/18/87	The Washington Design Center "Contextual Buildings"
09/20/86	McIntosh/Drysdale Gallery Exhibition of Drawings & Models
11/13/85	The Catholic University of America Washington, D.C. "Works" *Lecture/Exhibition*
10/13/84	Don't Tear It Down Tour of Architects' Offices
01/1981	Lunn Gallery Exhibition models and drawings

SELECTED COMMISSIONS

2002   **Mount Vernon Walk** Washington, D.C. Architectural design of the large, urban development won in a design competition with 11 development teams. Project includes over 500 housing units and 57,000 square feet of retail. The design provides affordable and market-rate housing, artists' live/work studios, a pedestrian promenade, and a live performance theatre.

        Nashville Symphony Concert Hall Nashville, Tennessee. Design of a new construction, 1,900-seat pure concert hall for the Nashville Symphony Orchestra. In association with Earl Swenson Associates and Hastings Architecture Associates.

        Parkway Center Master Plan Las Vegas, Nevada. Master plan for mixed-use development of a 61-acre site adjacent to downtown.

        Martha's Vineyard Residence Martha's Vineyard, Massachusetts. Design for a large, new, private residence on a beachfront estate.

2001   **Mount Vernon Walk** Washington, D.C. Architectural concept design for 400 housing units and 40,000 square feet of community retail for a development-rights competition for a 3.2-acre in-town site.

        Frisco AA Ballpark Frisco, Texas. A 10,000-seat, 24-suite, minor league ballpark for the Class AA affiliate of the Texas Rangers. This facility will serve as the focal point for the 70-acre Stars City development. In association with HKS.

        Arabian Horse Heritage Center Fort Worth, Texas. Planning and site design for a new museum.

        Stars City Master Plan Frisco, Texas. Master planning and site design for a new mixed-use development including a hotel, conference center, ice rink, and minor league ballpark.

2000   **Hawken School Master Plan** Cleveland, Ohio. Master planning and programming for a private middle and upper school on two campuses. Planning includes landscaping, building design, and location for the new and existing facilities.

        Frisco Square Phase I Buildings Frisco, Texas. Design for mixed-use buildings as part of a master plan designed by DMS/AS. The buildings include both apartments and office spaces over retail spaces.

        Hawken School Natatorium Cleveland, Ohio. Design for a 27,000-square-foot pool building that includes a new, shared lobby with existing athletic facilities and a competitive swimming and diving pool. In association with Collins, Gordon, Bostwick Architects.

        Frisco Square Frisco, Texas. The master plan for the 140-acre site calls for a mixed-use development and strives to emphasize pedestrian use through the inclusion of arcades and shared green spaces.

        Rhine House Restoration St. Helena, California. Restoration of the historic Rhine House Mansion on the Beringer Vineyards, using new wood casework that will delineate smaller spaces within the original volumes of the winery and will complement the palette of the original stone structure. In association with Architectural Resources Group.

        North Shore Housing and Garage Pittsburgh, Pennsylvania. Design for a new residential building and garage in the North Shore area of Pittsburgh.

        Cook Children's Medical Center Hospital Inpatient Expansion Fort Worth, Texas. A new 150,000-square-foot addition to the hospital, designed by DMS/AS. Contains rehab and neonatal units, patient room floors, offices, classrooms, and an auditorium.

        Parker Square Flower Mound, Texas. Design of two additional retail/office buildings that are part of a 24-acre Town Square master plan designed by DMS/AS. In association with Vidaud + Associates for Buildings 900 and 800.

        Southlake Town Square Phase II Buildings Southlake, Texas. Design for part of a retail and office building in the Southlake Town Square master plan as designed by DMS/AS. In association with Beck Architects.

        Private Residence Fort Worth, Texas. Renovation and minor addition to an historic home for a small family.

        Texas Rangers Master Plan Update Arlington, Texas. Revisions and expansion of the scope of the original master plan to increase pedestrian-oriented, mixed-use development adjacent to all sides of the existing major-league ballpark.

        New York City Apartment New York City, New York. Interior design and furnishings for a 3,600-square-foot apartment on Central Park West.

        Cook Children's Medical Center Outpatient Surgery Expansion Fort Worth, Texas. Design of additional emergency services and building expansion as part of the hospital's master plan.

1999   **Florida Marlins Ballpark** South Florida. Site selection, planning, and design of a major league ballpark for the Florida Marlins Baseball Club. The design envisions lushly landscaped tropical concourses and a unique retractable roof to maximize fan comfort.

        Tarrant County Law Center Fort Worth, Texas. Design for a 375,000-square-foot county court building that includes 28 Family and Civil District courtrooms. In association with Gideon/Toal.

        Cook Children's Medical Center Ancillary Services Building Fort Worth, Texas. A new 125,000-square-foot building to house Information Systems, Administration, and office space.

        The Presidio of California San Francisco, California. Design Advisors to the Presidio Trust for the conversion of the 1,480-acre former military base to an urban National Park.

        Southlake Town Hall Southlake, Texas. A new-construction, 80,000-square-foot city hall, housing both city and county functions along with a courtroom, city council chambers, and a new public library. In association with GSI Architects.

        Victory Plaza Dallas, Texas. Master planning and design of a two-acre urban plaza in Victory, an urban development in downtown Dallas. As a forecourt to the American Airlines Center, the development includes two five-story mixed-use retail/office buildings that surround the plaza. In association with HKS.

        Bank One Building Fort Worth, Texas. Design for a 12-story, 285,000-square-foot office building with an attached twelve-story garage in an urban setting offering retail space on the ground level, and loft-style office space on the other 11 floors. The building creates a link between the rich architectural past of Fort Worth and its high-tech business environment of today. In association with HKS.

Pittsburgh Planning Pittsburgh, Pennsylvania. Master planning for revitalizing a waterfront warehouse district. Included are new and converted buildings and a realigned street grid to reconnect the area with downtown.

Cook Children's Medical Center North Garage Fort Worth, Texas. Design for a new 600-car garage as part of the hospital's master plan. In association with Intertech Design, Inc.

1998 American Airlines Center Dallas, Texas. Design of 750,000-square-foot arena with seating for 20,000; new home for the Dallas Mavericks and Dallas Stars. The arena will be the centerpiece of 60 acres of urban development adjacent to downtown Dallas. In association with HKS.

280 Forest Drive North Haven, New York. Design of a 5,500-square-foot private residence on waterfront bluff. In association with William J. Reese, Architect.

Miami Intermodal Center Miami, Florida. A mixed-use waterfront development complex encompassing retail, office, hotel, residential, entertainment, and parking.

Cityplace Master Plan Dallas, Texas. Conceptual design for a master plan for a 31-acre track in Dallas for mixed-use office, retail, and hotel development.

Cityplace Office and Retail Building Dallas, Texas. Design for the first office building to be developed under the Cityplace Master Plan. Eight-story main building, two retail buildings, and 700-car garage. In association with HKS.

Cityplace Village Dallas, Texas. Conceptual design of a mixed-use residential and retail development in the Cityplace section of Dallas.

West Village Dallas, Texas. Mixed-use retail and residential development with 150,000 square feet of retail space, 200 condominium apartments and 700-car garage. In association with KSNG Architects.

Private Residence Aspen, Colorado. Renovation of a 19th-century dairy barn into a vacation home.

Guesthouse in Rocky Mountains Design and interiors for a new 4,200-square-foot log guesthouse.

Chateau St. Jean Sonoma Valley, California. A 5,000-square-foot new-construction hospitality center with a 1.5-acre formal courtyard at an historic winery. In association with Hall and Bartley Architects.

Stonebriar Dallas, Texas. Conceptual master plan for a large mixed-used retail and office development north of Dallas.

1997 Beringer Vineyards Master Plan St. Helena, California. Master plan for an existing 17-acre vineyard including renovation of visitor center, office, old distillery, and outbuildings.

Stag's Leap Vineyards Master Plan Napa Valley, California. Master plan for the improvement of a 38-acre vineyard and its outbuildings.

Southlake Town Square Phase I Buildings Southlake, Texas. Design for a two-block square surrounded by retail shops, offices, restaurants, and a new city hall. In association with Urban Architecture for Phase One.

1996 Southlake Master Plan Southlake, Texas. Twenty-year master plan for a new downtown that is based upon a traditional town grid. 2.7 million square feet of commercial development will be accommodated on the 130-acre site.

Maddox-Muse Rehearsal/Concert Hall Facility Fort Worth, Texas. 70,000-square-foot support complex for Bass Hall including rehearsal halls, studios, and arts organizations' office space. In association with HKS.

Texas Pacific Group Offices Washington, D.C. Design, furnishing, and finishes for a 4,000-square-foot office suite. In association with A.I. Boggs.

Worthington Hotel Ballroom Conference Center Fort Worth, Texas. Final phase of a three-phase project. 74,000-square-foot renovation of main and secondary ballrooms, meeting rooms, and lobby spaces to convey a regional flair. In association with Vidaud + Associates.

60 Auberge Road Napa Valley, California. Renovation/addition to a 1950 vineyard house. In association with More Associates.

Dallas Arts District Master Plan Dallas, Texas. Master plan for three blocks in the Dallas Arts District. Mixed-use development including residential, commercial, and entertainment facilities.

3465 Macomb Street Addition Washington, D.C. Renovation/addition to a private residence.

Severance Hall Cleveland, Ohio. Restoration, renovation, and 40,000-square-foot expansion of the landmark Severance Hall, home of the Cleveland Orchestra. In association with GSI Architects.

Fort Worth Public Library First Floor Interior Fort Worth, Texas. Over 50,000 square feet of finished interiors including grand lobby spaces, a children's library, and a multimedia center library. In association with Hidell Architects.

2710 Chain Bridge Road Washington, D.C. Library, kitchen, and master bedroom addition to a previously expanded Victorian-style cottage.

Cook Children's Medical Center Medical Office Building Fort Worth, Texas. Four-story 83,500-square-foot office building on the Cook Children's Medical Center campus. In association with FKP.

South Extension Fort Worth, Texas. Addition to main hospital block of Medical Center Campus, to include expansion of the cafeteria, conference facilities, and bridge connection to parking garage and medical/office building. In association with FKP.

Parker Square Master Plan Flower Mound, Texas. A 24-acre retail and office development organized along two main streets which front a traditional town green.

SELECTED COMMISSIONS

Western Heritage Center Fort Worth, Texas. Site selection and master plan for cultural complex including three museums.

Sid Richardson Museum of Western Art Fort Worth, Texas. Renovation of an existing public gallery and non-profit offices, including code upgrades and a new entry façade.

1995   **Chicago Bears Stadium** Chicagoland, Illinois. Architectural consultation to the Chicago Bears in their efforts to build a new 75,000-seat football stadium.

Private Lodge Rocky Mountains. Owner consultation and interior architecture and design for a 16,000-square-foot, new-construction log residence and caretakers' cottage. Includes selection, purchasing, and placement of furnishings and artworks.

Lake Las Vegas Henderson, Nevada. Development assessment and preliminary master planning for a 2,200 acre mixed-use development around a 320-acre man-made lake.

Barnes and Noble Bookstore Fort Worth, Texas. Interior design for a two-story 28,000-square-foot downtown bookstore and café. In association with Antunovich Associates.

Worthington Hotel Lobby and Restaurant Fort Worth, Texas. Phase Two of a three-phase project. Renovation of the main lobby and A Star of Texas Grill and Restaurant. In association with Huitt/Zollars.

Cook Children's Medical Center Central Plant Fort Worth, Texas. Central heating and cooling plant for the Medical Center Campus. In association with FKP.

National Cowgirl Museum and Hall of Fame Fort Worth, Texas. 40,000-square-foot new-construction hall of fame and museum in the Fort Worth Cultural District. In association with Gideon/Toal.

Yale University Environmental Science Center New Haven, Connecticut. A 96,000-square-foot laboratory, teaching, and storage facility for the Yale Institute for Biospheric Studies, a new interdisciplinary environmental science center. This building is an addition to the Peabody Museum. In association with GSI Architects.

1994   **Wells Fargo Building** Fort Worth, Texas. Design of a five-story downtown office building with bank, restaurant, and retail space at street level. In association with HKS.

Blockbuster Park Master Plan Team South Florida. Venue architects for arena and stadium components of a 3,000-acre sports and entertainment complex in Dade and Broward Counties, Florida.

Dinnerware Design Design of five patterns of porcelain china for Architectural Objects, Inc.

Preview Center at the BoardWalk Orlando, Florida. New-construction 26,000-square-foot clubhouse that will function as the central marketing facility for the Disney Vacation Club.

Disney's Wide World of Sports Complex Orlando, Florida. Design of a 6,500-seat field house and a 7,500-seat baseball park in a complex of varied sports venues. In association with HKS.

1993   **New York Botanical Gardens Library/Herbarium** New York City, New York. New-construction building to contain a 5.5 million specimen herbarium and botanical library. Includes renovation of portions of the landmark Museum Building for the public areas of the library.

Nancy Lee and Perry R. Bass Performance Hall Fort Worth, Texas. 2,100-seat performing arts hall to house the Fort Worth Ballet, the Fort Worth Opera, the Fort Worth Symphony Orchestra, and the quadrennial Van Cliburn International Piano Competition. In association with HKS.

Sundance East Fort Worth, Texas. Ten-theater multiplex cinema and 55,000-square-foot retail and commercial office space occupying a full downtown block. In association with HKS.

Corporate Headquarters Master Plan Fort Worth, Texas. Master plan for 1.9-million-square-foot corporate headquarters campus on 11 city blocks with seven separate buildings, a 280-foot long-span network control facility, and garage space for 3,000 cars.

Montessori School Fort Worth, Texas. New façade in De Stijl style for an existing building.

1992   **Shanghai/Cypress** Shanghai, Peoples Republic of China. Master plan and design of buildings on a 50-acre site including a 120-room hotel, 240 apartment units, a restaurant in a restored historic building, an athletic club, and 80 luxury villas.

New York Botanical Gardens Master Plan New York City, New York. Master planning for the further growth of the Botanical Gardens campus to accommodate a new Library/Herbarium, restaurant, catering facility, and visitors' center.

Mount Zion Front Royal, Virginia. Renovation and master plan of a 4,500-square-foot historic residence and 300+ acre site.

Worthington Hotel Fort Worth, Texas. Renovation and upgrade of 506-room hotel to Five-star level with new furnishings and finishes to convey a regional flavor. In association with Yandell and Hiller.

Oak Grove Marshall, Virginia. Addition to existing four-bedroom country house including new swimming pool and landscape.

Whydah Pirates Complex Charlestown Navy Yard, Boston, Massachusetts. 150,000-square-foot entertainment/educational facility dedicated to the history of pirates.

Cook-Fort Worth Children's Medical Center Fort Worth, Texas. Master plan and 120,000-square-foot addition including expansion of the cafeteria and conference facilities.

Fort Worth Public Library Fort Worth, Texas. 200,000-square-foot expansion and master plan for the central library. In association with Growald Architects.

1991   **Texas Rangers Ballpark Master Plan** Arlington, Texas. Master plan for the 300-acre site surrounding the new Texas Rangers Ballpark.

Texas Rangers Ballpark Arlington, Texas. Design for a 48,000-seat stadium complex. Commission awarded as result of nationwide design competition. Completed in association with HKS.

Rock Hill Farm Front Royal, Virginia. Renovation of a 5,500-square-foot residence on a 700+acre site.

1990   **Pentagon Square** Arlington County, Virginia. 1.1-million-square-foot speculative office space plus rezoning studies to include 50–80,000 square feet of retail and up to 120 apartments. Presented to G.S.A. and D.O.D.

I-395 Air Rights Project Washington, D.C. 1.9-million-square-foot office space, 250,000-square-foot hotel, 250,000-square-foot apartment building, mixed-use project originally submitted for the F.C.C. headquarters, revised for presentation to the G.S.A. for the E.P.A.

Sundance Eleven AMC Cinemas Fort Worth, Texas. Interior design of an 11-screen multiplex cinema. In association with HDR.

Sanger Lofts Fort Worth, Texas. Conversion of 75,000-square-foot department store to loft apartments. In association with Terry M. Harden Architects for construction-phase observations.

Sundance Master Plan Fort Worth, Texas. Urban center master plan for Fort Worth.

Penthouse Apartment Fort Worth, Texas. Custom 3,500-square-foot residence on two floors plus loft in Sundance West Apartment Building.

2853 Ontario Road NW Washington, D.C. 2,900-square-foot apartment renovation.

2601 31st Street NW Washington, D.C. Subsequent phase renovation of 1985 project, including 2,000-square-foot addition and numerous interior alterations.

1989   **Square 515** Washington, D.C. Mixed-use project of 290 apartments, 52,000-square-foot commercial and retail space, and a 6,500-square-foot community building.

Design for a Wedding Washington, D.C. Design for a wedding ceremony and reception space for 240 guests.

500 Park Avenue Penthouse New York City, New York. 8,500-square-foot two story apartment.

Natelli Woods Lane Avenell, Maryland. New-construction single-family residence of 17,300 square feet.

2215 30th Street NW Washington, D.C. "Art Gallery" addition to 20,000-square-foot private residence.

Mount Vernon Square East Square 515 Washington, D.C. Mixed-use project of 290 apartments, 52,000-square-foot commercial and retail space, and a 6,500-square-foot community building.

Jefferson Place/M Street NW Square 139 Washington, D.C. 400,000-square-foot office building and retail space in the central business district, incorporating existing historic row houses.

Square 185 16th and I Streets, N.W. Washington, D.C. 308,000-square-foot office building with views of the White House.

1217 Potomac Street NW Washington, D.C. Renovation/addition of 4,000-square-foot historic residence into gallery/office for a private art collector.

1988   **Hollywood Plaza** Hollywood, California. Urban mixed-use project of 1.4 million square feet including 1,000 apartments, office and retail space, and a health club.

1201 F Street NW Washington, D.C. Twelve-story, 238,000-square-foot new-construction office/retail building, with 69,000 square feet of underground parking. In association with Vlastimil Koubek and Page, Sutherland, Page.

1437 Rhode Island Avenue NW Washington, D.C. 400-unit new-construction apartment building.

Square 456/Hecht Company Building Washington, D.C. New-construction 240,000-square-foot office/retail component (of a 2-million-square-foot complex), retaining historic façades in the Downtown Historic District.

1987   **1301 L Street NW** Washington, D.C. 286,000-square-foot 12-story new-construction Planned Unit Development office building, with 90,000 square feet of underground parking.

1312 Massachusetts Avenue NW Washington, D.C. 200,000-square-foot/134-unit new-construction Planned Unit Development apartment building.

Sundance West Fort Worth, Texas. Twelve-story, 250,000-square-foot multi-use office/retail/cinema/condominium building. In association with HDR.

1133 Connecticut Avenue NW Washington, D.C. New-construction 227,000-square-foot office/retail building. In association with Vlastimil Koubek.

The Forum at Park Lane Dallas, Texas. New-construction, 310,000-square-foot retirement community. In association with Parker Croston.

2840 Woodland Drive NW Washington, D.C. Renovation/addition to an 8,300-square-foot private residence, originally designed by Clarke Waggaman in 1917.

4511 28th Street NW Washington, D.C. Renovation of a 5,200-square-foot private residence.

Mount Vernon East Washington, D.C. Master plan for a 1.6-million-square-foot phased commercial/residential development.

14th & F Streets NW Washington, D.C., the Westory Building. Design for new-construction, 162,000-square-foot office/retail building incorporating an existing 22,000-square-foot historic structure.

Square 247 Washington, D.C. New-construction 321,000-square-foot office building and conversion of an existing 85,000-square-foot office building to residential space, as Planned Unit Development.

17 Primrose Street Chevy Chase, Maryland. Renovation of a 5,000-square-foot private residence.

500 Park Avenue New York, New York. Renovation of a 1,800-square-foot apartment.

1050 15th Street NW Washington, D.C. Lobby redesign for a commercial office building.

3106 N Street NW Washington, D.C. Façade and garden redesign for a private residence.

1986   **The Saratoga** 4601 Connecticut Avenue NW Washington, D.C. 186-unit, 10-story new-construction Planned Unit Development apartment building.

555 Eleventh Street/The Lincoln Building Washington, D.C. 480,000-square-foot new-construction office/retail building, incorporating existing façades and located in the Pennsylvania Avenue National Historic Site. In association with Swanke, Hayden, Connell.

Pennsylvannia Avenue Development Corporation Lansburgh's Competition E Street NW Washington, D.C. 683,000-square-foot construction/renovation of a mixed-use development, including office space, apartments, retail, movie theaters, health club, and the Corcoran School of Art.

Square 698/1100 South Capitol Street Washington, D.C. 146,000-square-foot new-construction office building Planned Unit Development.

2424 California Street NW Washington, D.C. Renovation of a 9,000-square-foot villa circa 1900.

900 15th Street NW Washington, D.C. Façade redesign for United Mine Workers Building.

6832 Wilson Lane Bethesda, Maryland. Phase II renovation/addition to a private residence.

316 Houston Street Fort Worth, Texas. Renovation of a 5,000-square-foot office.

2213 M Street NW Washington, D.C. "City Cafe," a 2,740-square-foot, 100-seat restaurant/bar interior.

Law Offices Washington, D.C. Design for law offices.

5032 Lowell Street NW Washington, D.C. Renovation/addition to a private residence.

Square 166 Washington, D.C. New-construction 179,000-square-foot office/retail building.

415 Prince Street Alexandria, Virginia. Renovation of a 9,000-square-foot, 1802–10 "Governor's House" for a private residence.

2030 24th Street NW Washington, D.C. Renovation/addition to a private residence designed by Paul Cret in 1938.

2039 New Hampshire Avenue NW Washington, D.C. Renovation of a condominium in an historic apartment building.

2133 Wisconsin Avenue NW Washington, D.C. Feasibility study for the renovation of four buildings into a single office/retail mixed-use complex.

2960 Georgia Avenue NW Washington, D.C. Feasibility study for a 250,000-square-foot mixed-use office, retail, and residential planned-unit-development.

500 N. Water Street Milwaukee, Wisconsin. Renovation of historic seven-story warehouse for office use.

819 N. Marshall Street Milwaukee, Wisconsin. Renovation/addition of an 80,000-square-foot historic duplex for office use.

1451 N. Prospect Street Milwaukee, Wisconsin. Renovation of a 25,000-square-foot historic church for office/retail use.

3465 Macomb Street NW Washington, D.C. Renovation/addition of a 5,400-square-foot private residence.

1985   **Cook-Fort Worth Children's Medical Center** Fort Worth, Texas. New-construction 265,000-square-foot 169-bed children's hospital. In association with Karlsberger Architects.

2601 31st Street NW Washington, D.C. Renovation of a 6,800-square-foot private residence.

4922-A Saint Elmo Avenue Bethesda, Maryland. Redesign for an office building entry.

650 Pennsylvania Avenue NW Washington, D.C. Design for a 2,000-square-foot walk-in medical treatment center.

Westover Square Fort Worth, Texas. Design for new construction of three 2,800-square-foot attached speculative residences.

955 26th Street NW Washington, D.C. Design for a 2,300-square-foot custom apartment.

1984   **700 Chain Bridge Road** McLean, Virginia. "Merrywood" Renovation/addition of a 31,000-square-foot estate.

The Ulysses S. Grant House 3238 R Street NW Washington, D.C. Renovation of an historic estate for a private residence.

Central Park Master Plan Dallas, Texas. Land planning and architecture for a 42-acre, 3.6-million-square-foot, mixed-use development including office buildings, a retirement community, and a church.

Cooksey Drive/"Rosecliff" Seal Harbor, Maine. Renovation of a 10,000-square-foot vacation estate.

512 9th Street NW Washington, D.C. Renovation of an office-building lobby.

"Downtown Stages" Study of incentives for development of legitimate theatre in Downtown Washington, D.C., through the Washington League of Theatres.

Irving Shops Irving, Texas. Redesign of a 228,000-square-foot shopping center.

2871 **Tilden Street NW** Washington, D.C. Renovation/addition to a private residence.

955 **26th Street NW** Washington, D.C. Design for a 4,500-square-foot, ninth-floor penthouse apartment.

955 **26th Street NW** Washington, D.C. Design for a 4,400-square-foot, eighth-floor apartment.

River Hills Fort Worth, Texas. Land planning and architecture for 1,200-acre development.

Autobahn Imports Fort Worth, Texas. Renovation of Volvo/Porsche/Audi dealership showroom.

410 **West 7th Street** Fort Worth, Texas. Renovation of an office-building lobby.

Potomac Avenue NW Washington, D.C. Two speculative houses of approximately 2,500-square-foot each.

64 **Ocean Drive** North Shores, Delaware. Design for a new-construction 5,000-square-foot beach house.

1983
801 **Pennsylvania Avenue SE** Washington, D.C. Renovation of 50,000-square-foot historic Capitol Hill building for office use.

2319 **Bancroft Place NW** Washington, D.C. Addition to a private residence.

Westover Square Fort Worth, Texas. Master planning and site planning for a single-family housing development.

433 **Rivercrest Drive** Fort Worth, Texas. Renovation of a single-family residence.

1072-74 **Thomas Jefferson Street NW** Washington, D.C. Renovation/restoration mixed-use project in the Georgetown Historic District.

2710 **Chain Bridge Road NW** Washington, D.C. Renovation/addition to a 4,000-square-foot private residence.

1600 **U Street NW** Washington, D.C. Renovation/addition of 14,000-square-foot, commercial historic structures in the Dupont Circle Historic District.

Greensboro Plaza Fairfax, Virginia. Schematic design for a 400,000-square-foot, commercial office development.

Tysons Dulles Plaza Fairfax, Virginia. New construction of a 700,000-square-foot mixed-use development.

1982
650 **Pennsylvania Avenue** Washington, D.C. Penn Medical Building/Penmark Condominiums. 130,000-square-foot mixed-use development with office/retail/condominiums incorporating the Art Deco façade of the Penn Theater.

2007-9 **Massachusetts Avenue NW** Washington, D.C. Renovation/conversion of the 17,000-square-foot Alice Roosevelt Longworth mansions into office use.

The Griffin 955 26th Street, N.W. Washington, D.C. New-construction 134,000-square-foot, nine-story condominium apartment building.

3120 **N Street NW** Washington, D.C. Renovation/addition to a 10,000-square-foot private residence.

3252 **R Street NW** Washington, D.C. Attic remodeling for a private residence.

2350 **Foxhall Road NW** Washington, D.C. New-construction 18,000-square-foot private residence.

1981
1729-31 **Connecticut Avenue NW** Washington, D.C. Renovation/addition to two historic 16,000-square-foot townhouses for use as office space.

2011 **N Street NW** Washington, D.C. Townhouse renovation/addition to a private residence.

3222 **Scott Place NW** Washington, D.C. Renovation of a private residence.

1323 **L Street NW** Washington, D.C. New-construction 97,000-square-foot office building with a five-story atrium.

2110 **F Street NW** Washington, D.C. 70,000-square-foot, seven-story medical clinic.

1818 **N Street NW** Washington, D.C. 130,000-square-foot, new construction office building incorporating five existing townhouse façades. In association with Vlastimil Koubek.

Main Post Office Building Washington, D.C. Preliminary studies for renovation of the 725,000-square-foot Washington, D.C., Main Post Office Building into offices.

2100 **F Street NW** Washington, D.C. Ten-story, 65-unit condominium building.

1409 **31st Street NW** Washington, D.C. Renovation/addition to a private residence.

1200 **East Capitol Street, N.E.** Washington, D.C. Renovation of a 16-unit apartment building into condominiums.

1980
406 **7th Street NW** Washington, D.C. Renovation of a commercial building for major Washington art galleries.

2126 **Decatur Place NW** Washington, DC. Renovation of a private residence.

2213 **M Street NW** Washington, DC. New-construction 6,000-square-foot commercial townhouse.

444 **K Street NW** Washington, DC. Preliminary study for a 286-unit apartment complex with 137,000-square-foot of commercial space.

1691 **Q Street NW** Washington, DC. Preliminary study for a 19,600-square-foot new-construction loft space condominiums.

6832 **Wilson Lane** Bethesda, Maryland. Phase I renovation/addition of a private residence.

627 **E Street NW** Washington, D.C. Renovation of a commercial building.

SELECTED COMMISSIONS

1979   **Interstate Building** 418 10th Street NW Washington, D.C. Conversion of a 49,000-square-foot warehouse to office space.

Hanover Arts Project Unit Block of N Street NW Washington, D.C. Planned Unit Development of a 58,000-square-foot site.

1718 Connecticut Avenue NW Washington, D.C. New construction of a 35,000-square-foot commercial office/retail building.

1340 Vermont Avenue NW Washington, D.C. Conversion/renovation of a seven-unit condominium.

625 E Street NW Washington, D.C. Restaurant.

1312 9th Street NW Washington, D.C. Renovation of a townhouse into office space.

1735 Johnson Avenue NW Washington, D.C. New construction, 12-unit condominium.

1737-41 Johnson Avenue NW Washington, D.C. Renovation of a warehouse into 46 condominiums.

1700 Connecticut Avenue NW Washington, D.C. Renovation of a 17,000-square-foot commercial building.

1422 Euclid Street NW Washington, D.C. Renovation of a townhouse for a private residence.

1656 Irving Street NW Washington, D.C. Renovation of a townhouse for a private residence.

1726 Euclid Street NW Washington, D.C. Renovation of a townhouse for a private residence.

1310 Rhode Island Avenue NW Washington, D.C. Renovation of a townhouse for a private residence.

Foster Offices Washington, D.C. Design for law offices for an attorney.

Private Residence Beallsville, Maryland. Design for a private residence.

1978   **1722-24 Connecticut Avenue NW** Washington, D.C. Commercial redevelopment of an historic townhouse in the Dupont Circle Historic District.

408 M Street NW Washington, D.C. Renovation of a three-unit owner-occupied townhouse.

7713 Elba Avenue Alexandria, Virginia. Renovation/addition to a Charles Goodman–designed house.

1436 R Street NW Washington, D.C. Consulting architects for a 28-unit condominium.

1810-12 Ingleside Terrace NW Washington, D.C. Renovation of a 10-unit condominium.

1460 Q Street NW Washington, D.C. New construction condominium apartment building.

1615 Kenyon Street NW Washington, D.C. Design consultants for renovation of a 48-unit apartment building.

1734 V Street NW Washington, D.C. Renovation of a townhouse for a private residence.

626 E Street NW Washington, D.C. Renovation of a 12-unit apartment building.

Racquetball Club State College, Pennsylvania. Design for a racquetball club.

1219 East Capitol Street, NE Washington, D.C. Renovation of a townhouse for a private residence.

1809 Riggs Place NW Washington, D.C. Renovation of a three-unit apartment building.

1341 East Capitol Street SE Washington, D.C. Schematic design for a 24-unit apartment building.

903 M Street NW Washington, D.C. Renovation of a townhouse for a private residence.

1977   **Transition Offices** Washington, D.C. Design for the transition offices of a national politician.

203 3rd Street NW Washington, D.C. Renovation of a townhouse for a private residence.

201 3rd Street NW Washington, D.C. Renovation of a townhouse for a private residence.

Private Residence Washington, D.C. Landscape architecture for private residence.

Private Residence Washington, D.C. Renovation of a townhouse.

Private Residence Washington, D.C. Roof deck landscape architecture.

Private Residence Washington, D.C. Renovation of a townhouse.

1444 Corcoran Street NW Washington, DC. Renovation of a five-unit apartment building.

Law Offices Washington, D.C. Design for law offices.

1976   **Private Residence** Palm Springs, California. Private residence.

Flying Cloud Inn New Marlboro, Massachusetts. Conversion of a barn into a guesthouse and meeting rooms.

Private Residence Harper's Ferry, West Virginia. Conversion of a summer cottage into a private residence.

Shapell Homes Los Angeles, California. Redesign of existing house plans for Shapell Industries.

PHOTO CREDITS

Butler Inc.: 41 middle left and bottom left.

Charles Didcott: 143, 198/199 bottom, 206-209.

Dan Forer: 164, 166, 167, 169-173, 176, 177.

Tom Greene: 19 middle, 174/175.

Steve Hall, Hedrich/Blessing: 112, 114-117, 121 bottom, 122-124, 144, 146-151, 153, 155, 158-163, 183-189, 191-197, 198 top, 199 top, 200, 202-205, 210-215, 222, 223, 225-237, 239-243, 245, 244/245 bottom.

Hambright Hoachlander & Associates: 45 bottom right.

Jim Hedrich, Hedrich/Blessing: 20 bottom, 22, 24-26, 28 top left & bottom, 30 bottom, 32, 34-40, 41 top & bottom right, 42, 43, 46-48, 50-53, 56, 58-64, 66-72, 74-81, 92-94, 97, 98 top right, bottom left & bottom right, 99 bottom left & bottom right, 100-106, 107 bottom left, 109 top right, 110 bottom, 111, 118, 120, 121, 123 bottom, 125-127, 129-135, 138, 140, 152, 156, 157.

Anice Hoachlander, Hambright Hoachlander & Associates: 44.

Arnold Kramer: 18 top left and top right, 20 top, 30 top, 31 top, 141.

Michael Lyon: 107 bottom right, 108, 109 top left.

Maxwell Mackenzie: 82-86, 88, 89, 91.

Justin Maconochie, Hedrich/Blessing: 178, 180, 181.

Roger Mastroianni: 187 top left.

Dean Powell: 137 bottom right, 139.

Barry Rustin: 65.

SkyCam: 95.

Walter Smalling: 18 bottom, 19 top right.

Fred Sons: 16, 28 top right, 31 bottom.

David Stansbury: 136, 137 top and bottom left, 142.

David Wakely: 216, 218-221.

James F. Wilson: 37, 98 top left, 99 top, 110 top.